Praise for The Miracle Makers Club

"There comes a time in your life when you have to stop and ask why. And then someone like Dr. Joan Hangarter comes into your life. Now if you are like me, your initial reaction when you hear that a person is the founder of the Miracle Makers Club, you feel a little uncomfortable. You see, I didn't believe that miracles were for me or that they were happening everyday right before my eyes. What I did believe in was that people came into my life for a reason. Maybe it was time to look at life differently. Dr. Joan has changed my perspective and my life. But she didn't stop there. She created a place where people can come and find hope."
— SP, MA

"I am very aware of my true calling, and I wake up each and every day to fulfill that purpose. I believe that every person has a message to send to others. Dr. Joan has come to tell you that you can make miracles. I want you to understand the importance of getting on some spiritual path. It doesn't matter which religion you choose; just find one that helps your soul and seek to find answers to your many life's questions. If there's one thing I've learned in this life it's that when you're living your true self, miracles just seem to manifest."
— BK, L.A.

"Dr. Joan has gone from healed to healer; she becomes your partner in accomplishing miracles in your life by sharing the nuggets of her own life experience. She has been there herself."
— KK, San Rafael, CA

"Dr. Joan writes from cold hard experience. Her book is a treasure chest of practical tools, exercises, affirmations, and inspiring life experiences. You can only win big by working Dr. Joan's book for your own miracle life."

—Dr. GP, Marin County, CA

"Her writing is so clear and inspirational; she has made the recipe for miracles reachable for everyone."

—Dr. MK, Marin County, CA

"Dr. Joan has helped me to create many miracles in the short time I have known her. I can feel the pounds slipping away, and I feel lighter and freer to be myself by setting goals for my miracles and working towards them. The support and experience she provides is priceless. I encourage anyone who desires change in their life—but isn't sure how to go about it—to consult with Dr. Joan."

—AM, Victorville, CA

"Dr. Joan is an absolutely amazing woman who kept her feet on the ground when her life was in tatters. She has emerged from the chaos and reinvented herself completely, becoming a beacon for others, not only to handle adversity, but to teach others that they can become the absolute best. With the knowledge that she has, you can fly higher than you ever dreamed of doing."

—CF, www.speakersgold.com

The Miracle Makers Club

The Miracle Makers Club

is designed for people like me,

begging for a miracle to change their life,

hoping against hope that

things will dramatically shift.

Using these effective techniques to miracle making,

you can forget crossing your fingers.

Together, we can make it happen.

THE *Miracle Club* *Makers*

LIVE THE PROSPEROUS AND
SOUL-FILLED LIFE THAT YOU DESERVE

Dr. Joan Hangarter, D.C., M.S.
Founder of the Miracle Makers Club

Edited by Brooke Kelley

Published by
the Miracle Makers Club
P.O. Box 2527
Novato, CA 94948

Published by:
The Miracle Makers Club
415-883-0810
www.miraclemakersclub.com
P.O. Box 2527, Novato CA 94948
drjoan@miraclemakersclub.com

ISBN 10: 0-9745590-6-7
ISBN 13: 978-0-9745590-6-3

Library of Congress Control Number: 2006906420

Notice of Rights

Cover Art by Faith Ann Rumm, www.rummstudio.com
Cover and Text Design by Dotti Albertine, www.albertinebookdesign.com

Printed in the United States of America

This book is dedicated to my children—
the original founders of the Miracle Makers Club.
Thank you for trusting me, staying by my side,
and playing the miracle game in our time of need.
I am forever in debt to you ...
May our lives continue to unfold
in unlimited, miraculous ways.

And to everyone who is in need of a miracle.
May you find the strength within you ... to believe.
You have, within you, the ability
to live a prosperous and healthy life.
This is your miracle mandate.
You already are a miracle maker
and you've just become a member
of the Miracle Makers Club.

WELCOME

Special Thanks

My most important gratitude goes to my children, Anton and Elana, for giving birth to The Miracle Makers Club with me. Without your faith we would have never triumphed.

Thank you to the universe of miracles, which makes all things possible.

And to those loyal friends and family who encouraged my dreams and helped me to face my challenges, I am eternally grateful. I must acknowledge my wonderful sister, Hildy, and my brother-in-law, Gary, for being my numero uno support team no matter what. You never turned your back on us, even when you didn't understand. To Aunt Pearl for being my aunt through thick and thin. And to all my friends who remained loyal; from the bottom of my heart, you kept me alive. Bunny and Madeline, I will be ever grateful. Faith, you are a genius. Elizabeth you are my star, and Liz, you make my day go better. And finally, Lalo ... enjoy heaven!

A special acknowledgement goes to Ray Bourhis, Alice Wolfson, and Dan Smith for ensuring that justice and truth prevailed. Special appreciation to Corporate Crimefighters, Jim Mooney, Linda Nee, Doc Judy, United Policyholders, and others for their continued fight to help the victims of this insurance company.

My thoughts go out to all victims as well as claimants of UnumProvident whom have been unjustly treated. I hope my journey gives you hope and ideas to turn your situation and challenges into your personal triumph!

Thanks to my support team; you know who you are. Melissa, Dale, and Seth. Michelangelo, you have been a loyal visionary and Gail Muldrow, I love you. Jack Barnard, for your assistance in harnessing my vision. Faith, thank you for creating the artwork that expresses my soul's desire. And finally, thank you Brooke Kelley for the much needed edits.

Contents

IN THE BEGINNING

The *San Francisco Examiner* presents the Joan Hangarter story,
"IT'S TOUGH TO BE POOR, TOUGHER YET IN MARIN COUNTY"

Publication date: 12 / 19 / 2001

D<small>R. J</small>OAN A<small>BRAMOWITZ</small> H<small>ANGARTER</small> used to live and work in San Francisco. She was a chiropractor before she hurt her right arm. She got her degrees from Boston University, Long Island University and Los Angeles College of Chiropractic. Now she's 52 and a single mom. She lives with her two children, a girl, 11, and a boy, nine, in Novato, of all places. And now she is broke and struggling daily. Here is Hangarter's story in her own words.

In search of enlightenment, I moved from my native New York to California, the land of opportunity. I did well, only to experience a major catastrophe in my 50s, rendering me flat broke. I lost everything except my two children.

Now I am a member of Marin County's impoverished poor. While many of you have the luxury of sitting with your family at the dinner table with greens and arugula topped with walnuts and goat cheese and tossed in balsamic vinaigrette, my staples are Top Ramen and macaroni and cheese. I have a personal relationship with hot dogs and beans. I can pretend it is glass of chilled Chardonnay as I am sipping my overripe wine from my child's plastic cup decorated with trains.

For two years, my sole shopping destination has been The House of Safeway. I am determined to get the most for my $20. I need food as well as light bulbs, toilet paper, detergent and other such items. One-hundred and fifty bucks are required, not the paltry bill in my hands.

I have one treat, which I call my forbidden luxury. I am addicted to vanilla bean coffee that I must have with half and half. It is prohibitively expensive, but I rationalize that I cannot afford not to have it. My sanity depends upon having that cup every morning. Then I know that I am safe. At least for today.

Each month, on the ninth or 10th, I receive my allotment of food stamps, $230, to feed a family of three. That is $7.60 per day. Despite rationing, they are quickly spent. By week four, our diet is Top Ramen in the morning, Top Ramen in the evening, Top Ramen in the summertime! I cook for the children and have long since learned to ignore my hunger.

REAL PINTO BEANS

Some days, the refrigerator and the cabinets are empty. It can't be helped. The kids know when I cook the pinto beans and take out the tortillas that we are back on rice and beans. The first time I went to Human Needs, I requested pinto beans. I was handed a can of refried beans.

"No," I replied, following her into the storeroom, "I want pinto beans, the real ones." She replied, "These are reserved for the Hispanics. Caucasian women never get this." On my second visit, she said the exact same thing when I followed her into the storeroom. I left with several pounds of pinto beans.

I am scared 864,000 seconds a day. The grip on my heart never lets up. My worst fears have been realized. The sky has fallen.

I don't turn on the heat when I am cold. It is too expensive. Electricity is a luxury. I wear long underwear from November through May. Restaurants, theater and music are vague memories of the past. That was another person. That's not me now. Today I am a bag lady. I have nothing.

I cook for friends, and they buy the food. On those days, I cook a real meal, with greens, and chicken, and soups or desserts. I make everything from scratch. On those days, I am not a poor person in my gloomy kitchen. Fresh foods revive my spirits. I am cooking a real meal with real food for real people.

ONE OF 1.2 MILLION

In September of 2000, shortly after I went on welfare, or "cash aid" as it is called now, 1.2 million others were recipients of aid in California as well. I wasn't alone.

Sitting in the social service office, waiting for my name to be called, I was taking the final step of a series of humiliations, tragedies and setbacks. Without going into my story, from riches to rags, I lost my house, my car, all my furniture and belongings as well as all my clothes.

One day I woke up and there was no money. There was no food, and there was no place to go. I cannot go back to sleep and restore my wealth. My nightmare never ends.

It occurred to me that I had hit bottom when I took my

place in line at the Social Services Office. I signed permission slips to open the entire book on my life, to every government agency possible.

Last month my nervous breakdown was broadcast to Children's Protective Services. The social worker took both children from their classrooms to interview them about their life at home. I held my breath in fear until the worker completed the inspection of my home and announced me fit. Fit for whom? I no longer live a normal existence. We are on the fringe.

I am certain that I got off at the wrong train station. I don't belong here. If I could just figure out how to get back on the train ... But it is going too fast and doesn't stop for me.

I want you to know.

I want to share the experience with you. I want you to know how it feels to be without—in one of the wealthiest counties in the country.

POVERTY IS HUMILIATION

Poverty is wondering how you will ever be able to afford toilet paper or paper towels. Its saying goodbye to simple luxuries such as light bulbs, batteries, butter, shampoo and soap. I have heard of some people who ration toilet paper, allotting so many squares per visit to the bathroom. Sometimes it's easier to move the light bulb from room to room.

Poverty is feeling rich when you trade with your friends and score six rolls of toilet paper.

Poverty is constantly obsessing how I am going to spend the money I don't have and how I will make do with the money I do have. I never win. There are always far more needs than resources.

Poverty is trying to scavenge up eleven quarters to do a load of laundry and multiplying that eight times.

Poverty drains my vitality. I never have enough good healthy food. I cannot get vitamins, supplements, homeopathic remedies or herbs on Medi-Cal. Wellness and alternative medicine have no home among the poor.

Poverty is trying to laugh when my cousin in New York says cheer up, sit down and have a cup of coffee, when I haven't been able to afford coffee for weeks.

THE GRINCH THIS YEAR

Poverty is signing up with Human Needs because I am determined to give my kids a holiday dinner and a holiday present. It's swallowing my pride, because, if I had to do it just for me, I would skip Christmas.

I am the Grinch this year. I pace my tiny apartment in two left slippers, my Christmas present from Human Needs. My daughter cried with sorrow and frustration when we opened the wrapping on her beautifully decorated gift.

Poverty is the sadness on her face when I explained to her that this will be a very simple Christmas, and she will have to get by on love and music and song. And watching her pull out memories of former happier times when we were a family and had a house filled with fire and laughter. In those days, the refrigerator was always full. "Mama, will we ever be normal?" she asks. I have no answer.

Poverty is the acute sense of longing and nostalgia I get when I see the advertisements for the Nutcracker.

Poverty is driving a car without heat that shakes, rattles and rolls. I am grateful for my chariot and am desperately afraid to jinx my good fortune at having the car in the first place.

Poverty results in relentless worry about paying the rent with the threat of homelessness—real. The result is a jaw chronically clenched from grinding my teeth. Increased stress results in a lowered resistance to disease, and a weakening of the immune system. No wonder the poor are always utilizing the emergency room. With so few doctors accepting Medi-Cal, we have nowhere else to go when the clinics are closed.

POVERTY IS

- Poverty is never having enough of anything.
- Poverty is black and white. Oh, I forgot gray.
- Poverty is gratitude for the family that anonymously sent me a turkey dinner last year for Thanksgiving. I humbly thank you.
- Poverty is forgetting that I once enjoyed all the things I no longer have. It is like being an alien on a strange planet, always on the outside looking in.
- Poverty is watching Christmas pass me by.

Reprinted with gracious permission of the *San Francisco Examiner.*

PART ONE

FROM STRUGGLE TO HOPE AND UNDERSTANDING

CHAPTER ONE

HOW MY WORST NIGHTMARES CAME TRUE

*I*N THE SUMMER OF 1999, every worst nightmare came true: bankruptcy, poverty, homelessness, and fear. Truthfully, there were moments I identified with Job, wondering why God had forsaken me, as he was clearly raining down misery upon me. I figured I must have really pissed Him off big time.

Prior to this, I ran a successful chiropractic practice in Berkeley, California, the East Bay of San Francisco, for almost twenty years. I had done well for myself. My practice thrived. I owned my home as a single mother of two children and leased a luxury SUV with tan leather seats. I was on top of the world. I had everything--until I became injured.

Ultimately, a head on collision with a vehicle that ran a red stoplight ensured that I would no longer be able to perform chiropractic manipulations. I experienced severe arm and neck problems, and the excruciating, sharp pain prevented me working. It was clear I would no longer be capable of resuming my work as a chiropractor.

Fortunately, I had purchased disability insurance, years before, to pay me the equivalent of my monthly salary, if I could no longer practice chiropractic. According to our contract, i.e., my policy, I would receive benefits at least until age sixty-five, if this occurred. I was relieved to know that even though I could no longer practice, I was protected by this policy. The roof would not fall down on me. I was safe—or so I thought.

Around that same time, I began a relationship with an aggressive man who became increasingly agitated as my financial situation deteriorated. Once I could no longer practice, we planned a joint business venture to ensure that I could continue to have an income. Unfortunately for me, and despite the large sums of money I put into the business, we were not able to turn it into a successful enterprise.

In May 1999, a representative from the insurance company, UnumProvident, knocked on my door. He informed me that the company would no longer continue to pay my disability benefits. He then proceeded to inform me that I was not entitled to partial benefits or rehabilitation and training benefits. My case was successfully resolved as far as they were concerned. I was stunned.

Nearly every person in the U.S. is required to buy an insurance policy for one reason or another. We insure our cars, our homes, our health, our loved ones, our income, our businesses … You name it, and we have an insurance plan available to cover it. We pay the company—not for services or products—but for a promise. We pay them to promise that they will be financially responsible for our problems when and if something goes wrong. Insurance is designed to protect you against calamities of all kinds.

And here he was, this representative who so kindly came to inform me in person that the company I'd trusted to help me was going to let me fall flat on my face. In the three minutes it took for him to relay the bad news, my entire world collapsed. I no longer had a source of income, and I had long depleted my savings. I was penniless--and very scared.

The realization that I was flat broke after years of successful living crushed me. The last time I endured financial hardships was during my chiropractic school days while working as a waitress to finance my professional training. As a student with a future ahead of me, my Spartan lifestyle was minimally tolerable, because I knew it was a temporary calculated phase of my life plan. But this was unexpected, unplanned for, and devastating!

My worst fears had just come true. I was about to become homeless with my two children. Anton and Elana were only eight and ten-years-old at the time.

WITHOUT AN INCOME, gone was the rent and food money. Within days, I received an eviction notice and was informed I needed to vacate my home immediately. The sudden shock was too much for me to bear, and my universe shifted. I no longer owned a business. I had no income. No savings account. No home. My sole asset was my Shell credit card, most likely canceled in sixty days. I could purchase fuel for my gas tank and junk food for our stomachs. We were barely surviving.

My world fell apart. In seconds, I went from Dr Joan, successful doctor, to Dr. Joan, bag lady. Like Chicken Little, I was screeching, "the sky has fallen." I told my story to anyone who would listen.

The stress resulted in severe, frequent, anxiety attacks, creating shortness of breath, and a pounding in my chest mimicking a heart attack. I cried nonstop. Hopelessness replaced security. I was crushed. I couldn't understand how I had gone from being affluent, to losing everything. Worse, there was no solution or way for me to repair the damage. My destroyed life overwhelmed me.

Without my career as a chiropractor, I had few other skills and no profession. Physically, mentally, and emotionally recovering from abject poverty seemed an accomplishment lifetimes away from this psychologically wrecked woman. When my self-esteem could no longer handle the mounting losses, I disintegrated.

To make matters worse, my boyfriend didn't take my financial setback well, to say the least. He accused me of working for the FBI and the CIA, plotting to destroy his business and his life. I was the enemy and needed to be taught a lesson. He even went so far as to threaten to kill me if things didn't get better. He sat me down in the locked soundproof concrete studio he had built in our garage and proceeded to punch the wall above and beside my head. I felt my hair move as he skimmed the top of my head showing me what he might do the next time.

At first, I didn't know what to do. There was no money for me to get away from him, but clearly it was time to escape. During the eviction process, I hid boxes in my car and stored them at a girlfriend's house—my safe house. It was tough to do, because he hardly left our home. Still, I persisted. I knew at some point, I'd need to go on a moment's notice, and I would want certain things to already be out of our house when the time came.

Soon another girlfriend, Madeline, who had become my lifeline, mailed an escape check for $500 to the safe house, I was good to go. I bided my time until the morning on the Fourth of July, when he left the house to weasel money from a friend, to take us to the Marin County Fair. I quickly stuffed clothing, sleeping bags, and whatever else I could hastily gather into our SUV, now designated as my ERV, Emergency Rescue Vehicle. I urged my two young children into my Land Rover and drove for dear life to my sister's home in San Diego, seeking emergency shelter on Independence Day 1999.

I knew that it was easy to set goals and create success when one is feeling successful already. But it seemed impossible to do when I was destitute and depressed. Intuitively, I sensed that if I could maintain my positive attitude, all would be well, but the years of living with an abusive man had eroded my inner reserves as well as my self-esteem.

My kids and I instinctively knew we needed a miracle to rescue us from our frightening predicament. Without a miracle, it would be impossible to make the changes we needed. I had no clue as to how I would restore my family to normalcy, but I knew it was imperative. I had become too weak, and I felt powerless. By creating a circle of three, I decided, we would generate positive waves of energy that might help mobilize my resources.

I told the kids that we were going to create a club to help us make miracles so we could become safe and stable. We named ourselves The Miracle Makers Club. I was the president, Elana, ten, the vice-president and secretary, and Anton, eight, was the treasurer and activities developer. My children and I sat together and held hands. We began to chant "om" as each of us asked for a miracle. We did this every evening for many nights. During these sessions, we escaped our daily reality and planned for a new future. We created bold dreams, exciting adventures, interesting people, and a large global life.

The path to recovery lay in bringing my family together and forging a powerful and committed team. Rising from the ashes was a formidable task; one I could not accomplish without their enthusiastic support. Like the three musketeers, we pledged to be all for one and one for all. We were three survivors clinging to each other on our miracle raft in the storm.

That first meeting of The Miracle Makers Club laid the foundation for our future. Elana made me promise that once we had achieved miracles and restored our life, we would use our club to help others. The story of The Miracle Makers Club would become an inspiration to all. From the very beginning, we knew the path we were about to embark upon would lead us to sharing our story with the masses.

Several days after our first meeting, I returned to my sister's house for lunch, after probably the worst day in my entire life. I was experiencing severe pain in my elbow, neck, and arm. I noticed the *Wall Street Journal* on the kitchen counter and the headline caught my eye. It announced that UnumProvident (my insurance company) was being sued in a class action suit for fraudulent insurance practices. The writer discussed a situation so similar to mine that it caused me to immediately call the same attorneys mentioned in the article.

Ironically, no one in the household knew who placed that article on the counter. It just appeared—as if from nowhere. During this period in my life, I never read the newspaper. (I was already so miserable that I didn't want to know about the rest of the world's problems.) But there it was. Sitting there just waiting for me to find it. This, my friends, was no accident. I believe that by forming our club, my children and I stirred up our miracle brew. We had begun to invoke a positive change in the right direction.

Over the next few years, I realized that I wasn't alone. The majority of Americans live on the edge, one paycheck away from disaster. Homelessness, bankruptcy, and disease are real threats, and survival is a full time job. I've since discovered that even successful women fear they might become bag ladies. With economic and political instability increasing, survival is scary and poverty rampant.

As a single mother of two children, I was eligible for cash aid, food stamps, and Medi-Cal. To feed my family of three, I endured the humiliation of begging for goods at the food bank. I remember one rainy, gloomy, Friday at Novato Human Needs; I waited for an hour only to be informed by a callous, government employee, that just one sack of rotten potatoes remained. She challenged me to take it. As I examined the bag, my stomach heaved and I ran from the room empty-handed and hungry for the next three days.

Thanksgiving and Christmas were the hardest to endure. I stood in line to get a shopping bag of holiday foods and a turkey. While there, I saw many familiar faces of parents I knew from my kid's schools among the volunteers distributing the food. I stood humiliated, torn by the desire to flee and the dire need to stay.

Human Needs of Novato allowed my kids to choose a holiday present for me from among the donated gifts. That was the year I received two left slippers, and my daughter ran from the room on Christmas morning in tears. This confirmed my suspicion that God had forgotten me. I had been ostracized and left behind to die. I had so offended the universe that I was now living a miniscule, meaningless life.

In my former life as a doctor of chiropractic, I knew many medical doctors personally, but I was too embarrassed to be seen in this condition. And since very few private physicians accept and treat Medi-Cal patients, my health deteriorated until I found the free Marin Community Clinic. I was now a county patient.

Day to day survival became my full time job. Gone was the memory of Dr. Joan, teacher, consultant, and public speaker. My circle of friends and family couldn't believe my deterioration from a successful dynamic doctor to depressed, helpless bag lady.

A major miracle was required to avoid hitting rock bottom and landing in a homeless shelter with my children. I secretly felt that in the end, I would recover, if I held onto my belief in miracles. I had no choice but to believe.

Despite my despair, I enlisted the assistance of my children, designing The Miracle Makers Club to guide, strengthen, and encourage us to overcome the destitution that threatened to keep us captive for the rest of our lives. If we were to regain financial security, we had to develop a family plan to get us there. We needed a miracle, and it wasn't enough to cross our fingers and pray for rescue. Our desperate plight required a major game plan. Half hearted, non-effective strategies would leave us in this state for eternity. Success was imperative to improve our life. The alternative … unbearable. If ever anyone needed a miracle, it was the three of us.

ON FEBRUARY 4, 2002, our big moment finally came—or so we thought. A unanimous federal court jury awarded me 7.7 million dollars in a bad faith claim against UnumProvident, for fraudulently denying my rightful benefits and forcing me into destitution. But because they opted to fight the judge's ruling, our financial situation did not change. The *Examiner* nicknamed me "the welfare millionaire". Winning the trial was a psychological victory, but it wouldn't help my lifestyle for a good few years.

With the jury verdict in my hands, I returned home after the trial and shopped for groceries with my food stamps. The next morning, my picture appeared in several newspapers, alongside a story explaining what had happened. I ran back to the market with the articles as proof to show all the checkers that I had a reason to be on food stamps. Their opinion of me shouldn't have mattered but it did. Everyone on the grocery check out line cheered for me, while sharing their own disastrous insurance nightmares.

I continued to pray for miracles throughout my hard times. I never stopped asking for a miracle, for I knew that without one, I would be stuck in Dodge forever, if you know what I mean. Nothing helped. The more I begged, the further my pie in the sky retreated. Rescue appeared impossible.

I bargained with my heavenly figure. "I will follow the straight and narrow," I entreated, "if only you send me a miracle and rescue me from my miserable existence." I vowed to reform and do what the universe required of me. I would be a good girl, give up caffeine, junk food, and wine. I would jump on the wagon and be a better mother. I would write books and launch my speaking career to help and inspire others. I would become perfect—if only I could have my miracle.

Praying for miracles exhausted me. No one replied. I don't think God actually heard one word I said. If He did, He sure wasn't jumping up and performing my miracles for me. Nothing in my life changed, and in fact, conditions worsened. My despair increased, and I felt empty and anxious. I had failed.

In truth, I was not in the miracle making mindset. I was trapped in the doom and gloom. I was the victim, and life was a struggle from my point of view. There was no easy escape, and my failures were staring me right in the face each and every passing day.

And I was just one example of the many thousands of lives who were harshly affected by Unum. After a minister read my story online, he contacted me for advice. A man named Joey was severely ill and disabled, and he was seriously contemplating suicide to escape the ruin his insurance denial had caused.

Joey could not work, yet Unum had refused to pay his claim. He lost everything and was about to be evicted from his tiny apartment where he had been barely squeaking by. Joey was unable to leave his house because of his illness and was seriously depressed. He had asked this counselor to assist him to commit suicide. The counselor was disturbed and had major reservations. The reason for Joey's decision to end his life was not based upon his serious health condition; it was the horror, humiliation, and loss of home and money that followed the denial of his disability benefits. It was easy to relate to Joey's horror and suicidal thoughts. After all, I felt the same way at times during my struggles.

When I received the e-mail asking for help, I forwarded it on to several people on my Unum buddy list. Many claimants in similar situations came forward to help Joey, and we formed a support group for him. We sent letters of encouragement, arranged for social services to help him, and some even sent money. The local paper ran a story about Joey as well. Unfortunately, we were too late. Joey died within the week. The authorities claimed it was a natural death, but we all suspect otherwise.

For the sake of my family, and for all of the hundreds of thousands of people out there suffering, I refused to give up. I knew there was a secret to transforming my life, and I was prepared to do anything to find out how. If only I could just find the switch and turn it on.

To catch the miracle wave required a complete transformative shift in my body and my mind. I had to revitalize my sense of purpose and my life's mission. I had to develop an action plan.

I promoted workshops on creating miracles but nothing changed—not for me or anyone else. I gave my pep talk to others, but I lacked inner resources of my own. I designed workshops and flyers on miracles, but I couldn't find anyone who would believe me. How could they? I barely believed it myself. I placed a classified ad in the *Pacific Sun* (as inexpensive as they come) to promote my miracle coaching. The only response was a pervert in search of a miracle to improve his sex life.

I was no shining example of any acts of miracles. I was dressed in my bag lady suit—my stained navy blue baggy sweats with holes below the knees. I was too depressed to inspire and motivate anyone or anything.

One morning, I realized I was on the verge of giving up. I couldn't take my life any longer. I was miserable, depressed, anxious, and suicidal. I had had enough of life. If this was all there was, I didn't want to be here any more. I wanted to plan my suicide, but then I thought about my children. I knew if I killed myself, it would destroy my kids. They would never recover. Even suicide wasn't a viable option. I needed something else.

I turned to meditation and visioning. I imagined it was the end of my life, and I was sitting in a circle of angels, divine beings, reviewing my experiences on Earth. I informed them that I had failed. I couldn't handle it here. I could not accomplish the mission I had set for myself. I felt awful, ashamed, and humiliated. Circumstances had been against me. Although I used justification as my excuse, in my heart, I knew I hadn't tried hard enough.

As if on cue, these beings showed me the successes I might have had, if I had chosen to follow my path. The intuitive voices and visions had been right all along. Had I just but trusted them, I would have accomplished miracles upon the planet, for myself and for others. Had I just had faith.

When I opened my eyes, I under went a life changing cognition, and my world transformed again. That realization was a turning point for me. Up to that point, my vision had been outside of me. My recurring theme was that one day, in the future, I would lecture, speak, appear on TV, host radio and TV shows, and have a fabulous life inspiring and healing millions of people.

I had fantasized that the media would print and reprint my story. I imagined that an agent from Starz or William Morris would knock on my door and offer me a lucrative book contract, for the story of Dr. Joan going from poverty to miracles. It was a hard blow for me when I realized it wasn't going to happen that way for me. Instant fame was not in my near future.

This forced me to wake up and realize that if anything at all like this vision was going to happen, maybe I had to do more than just sit around, twiddling my thumbs, waiting for luck to strike. But in order for my visions to become real, I needed to pretend to myself, or act as if my dreams could really come true. Only if I created the steps and followed my own action plan, would I then be successful. It wasn't enough to be passive. Wishing and hoping weren't the way.

There was my miracle I'd been waiting for. I'd always imagined my miracle would come in the form of a check, but actually, it was a simple shift in attitude. I turned on my miracle activation switch.

In the same amount of time it took for my life to go bad, I realized what had to happen in order to make it go right. I finally discovered that it was time to get on with my life. I had been unhappy far too long. I now had certainty, passion, and the stamina to go forward. If it was meant to be, it was up to me.

I had been jolted with electricity like somebody had just flipped my switch from off to on. I was granted my miracle. I literally heard the Hallelujah chorus in my head!

THE TIME HAD COME to share my story and my vision with the world around me. I had dreamed of being a professional public speaker, and now I was compelled to act like one. I had to learn the steps it takes to give public speeches. I had always had the skills and the determination to accomplish my dreams, and now was the time to make it happen. No more waiting for the miracle to ring my doorbell. I had made weak and halfhearted attempts before, but today, I was aware that I was in control of my fate.

Miracles are an internal state of mind. The miracle was never outside me; it was within me the entire time. Doubts and fears are normal to an unbelieving mind; they need to be transcended. I had no choice but to trust one hundred percent, because the alternatives were unacceptable. Circumstances forced me to acknowledge the truth--that if I believed in myself, if I thought that somehow I really could have this dream, this vision of the future, then I had to act upon those beliefs.

I had to stop crossing my fingers and get to work. Crossing your fingers and begging for divine assistance is a bad sign, because it signifies that you don't really believe that change can happen for you. You are praying for something you know in your heart will happen to others but never to you. Crossing your fingers squeezes the life force from the miracle.

I was fortunate, because I was able to remember my purpose. I'd had this vision since I was thirty-one. I was here to heal and inspire millions. How, I did not know. But in order to find out, I was forced to commit my time, energy, and life towards listening to my intuitive self and following that voice, no matter what it looked like to others.

It was time to turn inward for my validation instead of relying on everyone else to tell me what was best for me. I began to hear the soft whispers of my inner voice, and I became more self-reliant. I focused inside of my being to hear my calling. I watched no TV and had few friends. I spent my time creating a new life and repairing the one I was in, so that it could be more functional. There is no force like a woman with a purpose.

I BEGAN MY EXPERIMENT towards making miracles tenuously, because at first, I wasn't completely certain that this would work. Was it really possible for my kids and I to create miracles in our lives by being part of a miracle making club? Did thinking about miracles and creating vision statements guarantee success? And most important, did I have a mission as I thought, or was this all a figment of my overactive imagination?

I was determined to act as if all answers were yes. After all, I would never know unless I tried. It was that simple. I just started walking and moving towards the unknown mountain peak, hoping clarity would part the clouds hiding my future. My motto became, fake it till you make it.

Each time I faced obstacles, I would imagine myself on Oprah, sharing the story of the founding of The Miracle Makers Club with millions of people listening as tears poured down my face.

In the beginning, people would ask what I do for a living, and I would be quite embarrassed. I could hardly spit out the words. In a hushed voice I whispered that I founded The Miracle Makers Club. I expected people to laugh at me, and I felt uncomfortable, reticent about sharing the miraculous with an unbelieving world. As a speaker, I found it easier to market myself in the success and motivation genre, rarely using the word miracle, since I was told the word alienated corporations and scared people off. They didn't know if I was involved in a particular religion or an occult.

Part of my vision included becoming a talk show host. In my minds eye I saw myself as the host of an internationally renown talk show with the focus on creating and activating miracles, but I've learned that not all visions manifest immediately. Some of them take more time to simmer or brew, as we say in the miracle world, than others, so I turned my focus on things that I knew how to make happen already. Since television wasn't yet a reality, why not practice on the radio? I could use the show as hands on training as I turned myself into a much listened to talk show host.

My weekly radio show, *Make Your Miracle Today,* broadcasts live weekly at www.health.voiceamerica.com on Thursdays, noon PDT. The shows are archived on my web site at http://www.miraclemakersclub.com. Hosting the show and interviewing my guests is the highlight of my week. I get my opportunity to spread the miracle message. I share my philosophy on Miracle Making 101 and interview fascinating and unique guests who share theories and experiences. Many of my guests believe in miracles. The shows we have done have been quite amazing.

I have officially emerged from the closet. I am no longer afraid to tell the world my mission.

By experiencing and enabling miracles as my life's work, I have come to believe that miracles do, in fact, exist. There is a miracle mandate, which states that within you lies the potential to live full, prosperous, generous lives with meaning.

I have good news for you: You too are a Miracle Maker. You have the skills, the innate ability, and the ingredients to brew your miracle whether or not you realize it. I'm not talking about having the ability to do this later or in heaven--but right here, right now, on Earth. If you pretend that miracles do exist, for just a moment, it is quite possible you too can have whatever it is that your heart desires. Force yourself to think larger and bigger than your day-to-day life.

Once you recognize that you can live a miraculous existence, you become a real live Miracle Maker. You now have the ability to change not only yourself but the entire planet. Waves of miracles, positive vibrations, and transformational energies will spread from the inside out.

How do I know these secrets work? What evidence do I have of the existence of miracles? I know because I've observed it firsthand. Last summer, I spent two weeks in Damanhur, the City of Light, in Northern Italy. I had the opportunity to do five live shows, including three on video. In Italy, I was referred to as *La Journaliste*. I took on a complete new identity with a different vibration. It was so much fun. This miracle occurred, because I paid attention to the intuitive clues.

As I write the pages of this book, I am struck by the constant transformation of my personal life. Seven years ago, I was desperate. But today, everything we asked for is manifesting. We imagined a house with a pool and a basketball court, and guess what? Now we have just what we created in our minds.

And I'm still dreaming and pushing those goals into reality. We created a list of famous people we wanted to see. Not too much long after I made my mind up that this would happen, I was twelve feet away from Paul McCartney and Heather Mills. What's more, her hairdresser loves The Miracle Makers Club and promised to get Heather on my show at some point.

I have learned that it is no longer beneficial for me to limit my dreams. I tell my friends that now it's no longer a matter of being on Oprah's show; I have raised the bar. I will know I have achieved my dreams when Oprah is a guest on my show!

Now I awaken most days at dawn, excited, enthusiastic, and passionate about working. Once there was no future, and today I am at long last creating my lifetime dream. I am busy transforming my misfortunes into fuel. My message is simple: If I can do this, anyone can.

You have the ability to do all of these things and more. The keys to your miracle are within you already. You are the miracle. All you have to do is suspend disbelief, even momentarily, and give it a try!

I know that many of you don't believe in miracles. You would like to, but you think it best to leave the miracle making up to God. That's certainly one way of doing it. (wink)

However, f you are tired of the life you are living and long to live a different life, then you will want to learn how to activate belief and act as if.

But there are several different types of miracles, and while there's one type of miracle that spirit or God alone has the power to create, you have the ability to create many different kinds.

Throughout this book, you will learn the true definition of a miracle, I will share with you insight into the different types of miracles and how we attract them, and you will learn that there is no dream to large; anything can happen. Anything.

By taking only three necessary steps, you will be able to start making positive changes in your life today.

If bag lady Joan can do it, you can too!

CHAPTER TWO

SO YOU NEED A MIRACLE ...
BUT WHAT EXACTLY
IS A MIRACLE?

O YOU WANT A MIRACLE? You *need* a miracle. Perhaps this would be the perfect time for something miraculous to happen. Like a white bearded, handsome God shining light down on you saying "Hello down there. I remember you. Here's an olive branch with your lifeline. Have this blank check and a gift certificate to Starbucks. Enjoy."

Wouldn't that be nice? A juicy ripe miracle every time we needed one.

So what exactly is a miracle? Each of you has a different idea of what a miracle is. Before this point, you might have believed that miracles are only random acts of God.

For some, a miracle is an unexplainable act that no human could possibly accomplish alone. Or maybe you simply define a miracle as, "something that can never happen to me."

If your definition falls into one of these categories, or something similar, I am challenging you to set aside everything you've been told and consider that there's something more to miracles that you've yet to learn.

The word miracle has been applied to:

- Saints, healings and bleeding statues
- Synchronistic events
- Avoiding a near fatal crash
- Intuition
- Sudden insights
- The discovery of light
- A new baby
- Falling in love and staying in love
- Hope
- A helping hand
- Magic
- Winning the lottery
- Getting an education
- Being surrounded by loving families
- Food when you are starving

So you see, a miracle is not necessarily an unpredictable act of God. There are so many types of miracles that if you opened your eyes, you could see miracles twenty four hours in a day. In truth, you already have the miracle gene within you, thus you are a Miracle Maker whether you know it or not.

Before you get into the core of how to create miracles, I think it would be best to define the miracle itself. After all, if you don't know exactly what it is, then how can you begin to put it into action?

According to one dictionary, a miracle is "any amazing or wonderful occurrence." Another dictionary says, "A miracle is a wonderful thing, a remarkable example or specimen." The Latin word, *miraculum*, means to wonder or marvel.

In its very basic definition, that's all a miracle is—something amazing. Can you create something amazing? I want you to stop and think of three examples of something amazing that you have already created. My list includes my two children and this organization—The Miracle Makers Club. What is on your list?

1. _____

2. _____

3. _____

See! I told you that you are already a miracle maker! And since you have just recognized that you have already created miracles, this means that you have the power to do it again. And if you were already doing it, before you even knew what you were doing, just imagine what you can do when you *know* that you have the ability.

Last week I overheard a man in line at the post office discussing what a miracle it was that he received this letter in just three days, when once it would have taken three weeks, or even three months. We use the word miracle to describe any event that we find amazing. And now that you know the secret, let's break it down. There are four—yes four—different kinds of miracles.

MIRACLE A: MINI MIRACLE

You probably experience the first type, the mini miracle, quite often without realizing it. These are daily events, such as finding the perfect outfit to wear to the function just in the nick of time or receiving an unexpected check in the mail for $20. Miracles don't necessarily have to be a huge life altering, make Headline News, you're-not-going-to-believe-this event. Miracles come in all sizes and shapes. Look for the baby miracles; tiny, small rays of sunshine in an otherwise stressful day

When I was destitute, my miracles were simple, such as finding spare change hidden in my pockets when I had just run out of money for food. A miracle was getting a ride to and from school for my kids during the rainy season when we did not own umbrellas, raincoats, or hats. I walked two to three miles a day in the chilly San Francisco rain until my close friend Lalo couldn't bear to see me take another step. He bought me a beat up, salvaged 1981 Volvo that spit fumes. To me, the car became my Golden Red Chariot—my miracle car. It didn't matter that the roof leaked and the car had no heat. It ran. We had transportation, and that's a miracle.

Thanksgiving and Christmas were celebrated when we miraculously received gifts of turkey and trimmings. A neighbor knocked on my door with a made up story about winning an extra turkey at work. A mother from the school handed me a gift certificate for a ready-made dinner, complete with stuffing. Believe me, you could never convince me that miracles don't exist, because I experienced them even during the bleakest of times.

What constitutes as a miracle to one person may go unnoticed by another. A few cents for food and a beat up Volvo might be a curse to an affluent family, but to me, they were blessings. At the time, a simple turkey meant survival for another few days.

It is easy to overlook or discount the little events as they occur. That's why I call everything that is positive that comes my way—a miracle. I never leave anything out, because I want a steady stream of wonderfully nice things happening to me every single day. And when I take the time to record them in my miracle journal, I seem to attract even more.

The moral of the mini miracle is to never take anything for granted. I find that when I don't pay any attention, my power to create, declines. But when I track them and flex my miracle muscles, I become a magnet for events that uplift me.

When I do tune into my abilities, I have observed that I go from experiencing mini miracles once in awhile, to mini miracles on a regular basis, and finally to creating them *every* week. And once I honed my skills and conquered the mini miracle so that it's second nature, my abilities increase. I am then able to create something larger than myself.

MIRACLE B: THE "LUCKY" MIRACLE

The second type of miracle is what some consider luck, good fortune, or sheer coincidence. For instance, you might say that if someone wins a car, they did it completely by chance. If you pick up the phone to call your sister, and you hear her voice before you dial, this could be a coincidence. When you find a front parking space at Costco on a Saturday or if you catch all green lights on your way to work, you might be considered lucky. In fact, anything that's too good to be true, we reason, *must* have been a case of good luck. After all, that guy did it where others did not, and how *could he* have control over *that?*

What many successful people already know is that they have control over their destiny—even when it comes to winning the lottery. They know that they have the power to create their lives, just as they like it. To become lucky, in the real sense, is to become purposeful, mindful, and intuitive, listening to yourself and going with your own sense of rhythm towards a destination. Individuals who are consistently lucky have a disciplined and focused approach on the inside. They are usually following a quest, a voice, an intuitive gut feeling, and they are focused on seeing it through. They have created the mindset and the soil where they will soon grow their miracle.

Allow me to let you in on a little secret: *The universe will send us what we ask for.*

I classify it as a miracle, because as you create this aura of winning, sometimes it appears as though the good luck occurs at just the right time, when actually, it's you making it happen the entire time, know it or not. And *that's* amaaaaaaaazing!

One of my radio show guests calls himself Dr. Lucky. Randall Fitzgerald has devoted a lifetime to researching the qualities that lucky people have in common. In his book, *Lucky You,* he says, "If we recognize and appreciate the appearance of serendipity and synchronicity in our lives, we seem to enhance our chances of being blessed with good fortune. To some extent, there seems to be a law of attraction at work here—the more we notice something, the more we attract it into our lives." He believes that if you accept the miraculous you will have the blessings of good fortune. In other words, luck is nothing more than an attitude.

This is important, because winners who consistently win, tell us they get into an altered consciousness, a flow during which everything comes to them. Success isn't just by accident; lucky people create it from their mindset of prosperity. You have heard the saying, "success breeds success"? Spend time with positive, prosperous friends and you will walk away feeling naturally good.

Consider this: I was standing behind a handsome younger man outside the bathroom on a Southwest commuter flight. Just that morning I had expressed a need to find raw foods. Three hours later, I meet a man who runs a company that imports raw foods from third world countries and markets them to major natural food stores. Synchronicity of events occurs all the time. When you say to your friend, "I was just thinking of you, and here you are at the exact, precise moment I am," that's amazing, and that's a miracle, and you created it.

Don't believe me? You don't have to take my word for it. I'm not here to convince you of what I already know. I am here to provoke you to try it yourself. So what is it that you most want to happen? Want your favorite song to come on the radio—without calling the DJ? Want that coveted front parking space at the mall? Want to know that your sister's about to call you, moments before she picks up the phone? Seriously. All you have to do is decide. The universe is waiting to serve you a ripe, juicy miracle on a silver platter ... or gold, if that's what you desire. It's all up to you.

MIRACLE C: THE TRANSFORMATIONAL MIRACLE

The third type of miracle is the life changing, transformational miracles that lead the people involved to completely change their focus and life direction. This type is further broken down into two different categories. First, we have the tragic events such as accidents, illnesses, divorce, or job losses that force the person to reconsider the options. This transformational miracle, born from crisis, is a potent yet unwelcome friend pushing us along to uncover our true life's purpose.

I am a living example of this, and there are many others like myself. For instance, Mike McGauley lost the use of both his legs when a drunk driver hit his car. His doctors insisted on amputating his legs but he refused. He was determined to walk. Mike said, "the accident that almost killed me, turned out to save my life." Twelve years later, he ran his first triathlon and has gone on to become a professional speaker, coach, and founder of the Dream Builders.

Then there are people like Heather McCartney. She lost her leg as a result of a motor vehicle accident. She didn't run and hide like some. Instead, she turned her tragedy into a miracle. Even while in the hospital recovering from her own amputation, she became an advocate for amputees and artificial limbs.

Last summer, I heard Wesla Whitfield, a renowned jazz singer perform at a fundraiser for disabled children. I was surprised when she rolled onto the stage in a wheelchair. At a young age, an automobile accident left her paralyzed. She didn't let that stop her. Her performance was passionate, riveting, and held me spell-bound.

These stories, while miraculous and fascinating, are not entirely unique. Simple people do amazing things everyday. My mother experienced a miracle as well. She lived with me for the last eight months of her life, as her lung cancer rapidly spread. One weekend, I brought mom to the emergency room. Her oncologist advised me to call my family to her side, because her death was near. I called my friend Dr. Awender, an old school chiropractor. Dr. Awender adjusted one bone in mom's neck and told her that he had turned on her body's healing power. My husband and I went for Sunday brunch down the street at the Santa Fe Bar and Grill. When we returned to the hospital, my mother was sitting up in bed, demanding to be released.

And this wasn't her only miracle. One day she told me she almost died. "I went through a rather immense glowing tunnel towards a blinding light. There were magnificent radiant beings on both sides. They asked me if I was ready to come home. I told them no, because I still needed to reconcile with my sister, Pearl, and my daughter, Hildy." According to my mother, her body became as light as a feather. The pain disappeared, and she experienced an extraordinary sense of love and comfort. She was granted permission to return to her body, in order to mend her relationships—her last and likely most important mission in life.

Mom finally died when she was ready to go. She held my hand in my home while we listened to her favorite music. From that tragic, near death experience, she recognized that she had some work to do. Her purpose at that point was to make peace, and she was best able to understand and get moving on that path after this miracle.

She didn't fear death, because for several months she would awaken each morning having dreamed of her relatives who had passed on. Mom would describe the parties and events she attended in the dream state and assured me that they were all waiting for her

I believe that the universe works in mysterious ways. There was no possible way that I was going to get off my comfy couch and start the Miracle Makers Club as a healthy, somewhat happy chiropractor. Why would I? Where was the motivation? I had everything I ever needed and wanted. Without my tragedy, it's safe to say that I would never have the opportunity to heal and inspire millions. I wasn't following my life's purpose, and so the universe had to give me a good, hard kick in the butt to get me there.

There are some people, however, who have discovered their life's purpose without the pain and suffering. In this category is where you'll find the self-made millionaires, business moguls, and extremely successful people who have managed to create the transformational miracle, minus the tragedy.

Marc Allen is the quintessential new age self-made millionaire who symbolizes everything there is to know about positive transformational miracles. His success came slowly but steadily as he built upon his foundation of inner strength and knowledge.

Always a spiritual seeker, Marc spent many years studying Eastern philosophy and giving workshops. He even formed a new age rock band. At the age of thirty, on his birthday, he experienced his transformational moment. He asked the question, "what should I do with my life". That answer came in the form of imagining what his life would look like in the future, and he began creating in his mind the life he wanted to live. He realized he wanted to write books, write music, and start a company that would market and publish his work.

He went on to form the successful New World Library with Shakti Gawain, whose very first book, *Creative Visualization*, has sold over three million copies. Mark's first instrumental album, *Breath,* sold over 100,00 copies. He has become an inspiring speaker and written books on the topics of visionary business and visionary life, New World Life publishes books on self help, body, mind and soul, a collection that changes lives.

I might consider Erin Brokovich, a single mother of three, to be another example of a transformational miracle. In case you haven't seen the movie (based on a true story), I can explain. Erin discovered medical records in her boss's real estate files. Wondering why medical records were mixed up with real estate, her preliminary interviews uncovered the secret of massive groundwater chemical pollution that was being created by Pacific Gas and Electric Company in Hinckley, California.

TAKING ON A LEGAL CASE AGAINST PG&E and uncovering the truth about the contaminated groundwater was a daunting undertaking, to say the least. To win such a case you must be determined, committed, and willing to do what ever it takes to uncover the truth—no matter what. The people who drank the polluted water wanted answers to why their families were becoming mysteriously and chronically ill. Erin was instrumental in uncovering what they wanted to know and the case has become a landmark case for other plaintiffs. Erin became larger than herself, she transformed, and because of her, claimants were compensated for their ordeals and medical nightmares.

She wasn't afraid to take on a giant corporation. Her tenacious investigation led to the largest settlement ever for a class action lawsuit. Having been involved in the legal system I understand that this is a major miracle..

If you haven't already started moving towards following your life's intended path, I urge you to get there on your own (with the help of this book, of course). Don't even give the universe an opportunity to do it for you. Just make up your mind to do it, and then go do it.

Like these fascinating examples, your own obstacles and challenges can become the fuel for your life transformational miracles. Step away from your problems, and reconsider them from the higher perspective. What life lessons are you learning from this? What do your challenges represent? What is the message in this challenge for you to overcome? This becomes the fertilizer to grow your miracle. Grab hold of the opportunity to make change before life does it for you.

MIRACLE D: UNEXPLAINABLE EVENTS

I call the last type, miracles of the fifth dimensional kind. They are the result of extraordinary, unexplainable events that normal science and rational explanations cannot answer. For instance, one example is the statue of Mary who cries tears of blood. Both Jesus and Mohammed fed masses of people with only a small amount of food. Jesus walked on water and cured the blind. Joan of Arc had visions that she was to lead an army to crown the prince. These types of miracles are the ones that have been sanctioned by the Catholic Church.

Even in the Jewish collection of laws, there are descriptions of miracles in the *Talmud*. An old Jewish proverb says: "He who does not believe in miracles is not a realist." (These books even discuss the miracles that we *can* control and create. They are designed for people who want to learn how to harness and create their own miracles.)

Myriads of unexplainable events have been recorded and studied for eons, and so far, to my knowledge, man has not yet learned how the average Joe can create them. But not to worry. So you can't create the fourth miracle. At least you now know that you have the ability to create three other types. In this book, we are going to focus on how you can create the mini miracle and the (positive) transformational miracle.

MOTIVATION TO MAKE MIRACLES

I will show you how to develop your life purpose and create your own miracle team. My vision is to bring together others who share your determination and commitment to success. The energy from the group consciousness enhances your power to the point where you will catch your miracle wave. Together, we will mix the miracle brew and activate the nutrients to get it going. Join our team of Miracle Makers. We will be your miracle buddies and cheer you on to success as you overcome obstacles and habits that sabotage your progress. Here, you will learn to formulate action plans to achieve your own tiny and massive dreams.

Don't be surprised if you awaken in the mornings, ready to leap from a deep sleep, filled with passion and excitement. Finally, you are living the life you yearned for, the one you prayed that you could create and have—if you only had that miracle you've always dreamed about.

What major miracles have happened to you already?

Try to think of a time when you experienced a Major Miracle. Have you created amazing events that seemed too good to be true?

_____

_____

_____

_____

_____

What life changing miracles have happened to you?

_____

_____

_____

_____

_____

_____

What other random miracles have you experienced?

_____

_____

_____

_____

_____

Don't worry if your lists are short. Mine were too when I first got started. If you have little or nothing, just know that you have the ability change that. We all fell in love with the story of Aladdin, who found a genie in the lamp. The genie promised to grant him three wishes. If I ask you what you'd wish for if you had three wishes, you'd likely outsmart me and make your first wish for a million more wishes. This is not only a good thing, it should be done by everyone on the planet.

If you could make just one miracle happen in your life, what would it be? For this question, try to focus on *the most important* miracle that you'd want to make come true.

_____

_____

_____

_____

Now that you're in the mood for making miracles, it's time you learn how to do it. There's an exact formula, and when applied correctly, your success is guaranteed. Are you ready to learn all about it?

∽

CHAPTER THREE

ASSESSING YOUR
CURRENT SITUATION

*Y*OU CAN CREATE MAJOR LIFE transformations in just a few different steps. The first thing that you must do, before you go anywhere, is to figure out where you are now.

I have a very close friend whose life is seriously challenged. She was forced to leave a small moldy cottage and move into smaller quarters, sharing a room in a house with raccoons. She blames her downfall on Bush's governmental policies that caused higher unemployment, but from the outside looking in, I'm thinking, "we all have the same president, and other people lost their jobs too. But they're not living with wild animals."

Thinking I could help, I suggested that if she started to take care of herself physically, and if she created more positive thinking patterns, she might find a better job. Had she focused on this, I'm absolutely certain she would have created success. But she was content to wallow in self-pity.

She was furious at me for "betraying" her by suggesting that her solution lay within. But don't kill the messenger. I was just trying to help. She didn't want help though. She wanted me to play along with her blame game and pretend she had no control over the situation. Until she understands that she is keeping her miracles far away with her continued negative thinking, nothing will change for her.

Despite my aggressive approach, I am still sympathetic to her plight—we can all fall prey to the clouds of self-doubt and victim consciousness. For years, I expected my knight in shining armor to gallop through the green woods to rescue me from my mundane life. In the midst of my nightmarish existence, I held fast to this hope. But I eventually had to come to terms with the fact that no one was on his merry way to save me. I finally had to save my own dang self. And that's really the only way it can be done. The only way out, is through.

Think of it this way, if your DVD gets jammed and you call up your friend, Fred, and he comes over to fix it, what have you learned through this process? When the VCR gets jammed again, what are you going to do? Well you're going to call up Fred, of course. And if Fred is on vacation, but you *really* want to see *Ghost* for the billionth time, what ever are you going to do? Maybe you could just go buy a new DVD, but in life, trading in your problems for a newer model—is not an option.

But if your friend taught you how to fix it yourself, or if you read the manual, or if you would have sweat it out just that once, you'd have the knowledge for yourself. You'd be prepared to face any issue that came up with your DVD ever again.

Well fortunate for you, I have taken the liberty of writing

the manual on miracles. After a lifetime of making mistakes and then learning to leap over tall buildings, I have created a comprehensive guide to teach you how to make your own miracles. This personal miracle handbook will guide you so that you'll know how to brew your own energy and transform your own life. Are you ready to learn how this all works?

SOCIETY SAYS

Our society discourages individualism. At an early age, we are in awe to learn that no human is like another, but as time goes on, we mock our neighbors for their differences.

You are encouraged to live within certain set guidelines and standards. Thinking outside the box is something you discover on your own, since mediocrity is the norm. The educational process, the media, and parental expectations attempt to stamp out your unique self-identity. You are trained to not listen to your inner intuition. Don't trust your inner sense of knowing. Don't believe yourself. From birth, you are programmed to put away your foolish dreams and replace them with a sensible life. Society demands that you perform according to its standards, and it is hard not to follow suit.

As a child, I was a sensitive, shy, and emotional. My father would yell at me, "Feelings? Who gave you the right to have feelings? I'll tell you how to feel."

Don't you love my dad's classic philosophy!? "There are two ways to do things: the right way and the wrong way. And there is only one right way which is my way. It's a rather close-minded look at life and people.

We are trained not to be different. In *Art and Fear*, authors David Bayles and Ted Orland tell us that "Nature places a simple constraint on those who leave the flock to go their own way—they get eaten." Too many of you live a life that others have planned for you. Society wants you to choose the temporarily easy route. If you don't buck the system and you follow orders; if you play by the rules, everything will be okay. In essence, you submerge your unique identity and don't listen to inner self—that part of you which knows the real truth.

My father gave me two options when I graduated high school. I could get a job, or I could go to college and become a teacher. Why a teacher? So that I could have babies, and then take the same vacations as my kids. Choosing my own future wasn't an option. Remember I told you I was timid, right? Well, I flunked student teaching, because I was too shy to stand in front of a group of seventh graders and give a lesson plan. I had to beg my advisor to give me a D for my student teaching program in order to graduate with my class. I was not cut out to be a teacher of middle or high school students. What's interesting is that if my father would have just let me be, he'd learn, years down the line, that there was a teacher in me after all. But some people cannot be pleased, and it's not your job or my job to make efforts to appease them.

The result of society's training is to become remote, mechanical beings, content to go to work for someone else and raise 2.3 children. It becomes near-impossible to hear or access your inner voice and your dreams slowly die.

Disney inspired my childhood with their theme song, "When you wish upon a star, makes no difference who you, when you wish upon a star, your dreams come true." As we mature, negative people stamp out the dreamer in you, and it is replaced by pragmatic realities of survival and life style. Society mocks the dreamers. Those who break through this negativity are the underdogs who are later celebrated for their vision, their brilliance, and their contributions. Very ironic, isn't it?

It takes courage to be different. I am giving you permission to let go of all preconceived notions and expectations from others. Take your disability, your challenge, your victim stance, and turn it into the fuel you need to fire your passion.

I once asked my uncle for a loan to help put me through chiropractic school. I erroneously assumed that because he was my deceased father's older brother, he would want me to succeed. Boy was I wrong. He chewed me out for changing careers at 26 and argued I should be working in downtown L.A. as a secretary, looking for a husband. I seethed inside as he told me I would never be a millionaire. That anger stirred me to be successful as a chiropractor years later.

People internalize adversity and hardships in a variety of ways. Some sink and fade. Others use them as fuel for change. Instead of bemoaning fate, ask why you unconsciously allowed this to happen. Look for the higher message involved. Maybe you were living a negative lifestyle because you felt you had to, and just maybe, it was time to stop and go down a different path.

I lost everything so that I could get to this very point in life that I have described to you. Without prodding, I wasn't going to go out on a limb and teach the secrets of Miracle Making. Not me. I was forced to sink or swim, take a deep breath and dive. My life was so unbearable that I was forced by my circumstances to change, kicking and screaming. I had no options because the alternatives were unthinkable. In my case, I could not imagine continuing my life as it was going.

It takes courage to be free. While the riverbank seems safer, your best option is to dive—immediately. It really is best if you move forward no matter how scared you feel. The bridge is shaky here, and you have nothing to hold onto. It is within this shift from the old world to the new, the unseen bridge between outer reality and inner certainties, that you will uncover your miracle. Don't wait too long or the flow of the river will swiftly change, the energy will shift and you won't catch that transformational wave.

You may see a tiny raft, your way to freedom, but when obstacles suddenly appear, you might think you need to run back. That's your old self-trying to trap you once again. If you turn back and go home, you feel like your bid for freedom was lost. It becomes that much harder to break free. Maybe next time you won't even have a raft. It's better to do it all at once as you go forward, without allowing the past to hold you back. Escaping from the illusions of your troubles and struggles requires a willingness to take risks.

Miracles are a matter of precise timing. That old adage, "you snooze you lose" is over stated only because it's true. If you forever dabble your toes in the water, you transmit to the universe a halfhearted, mixed message. You are neither in nor out; you are poised for a hasty retreat. Should things not work out as you hope, you have left yourself a fail-safe zone for retreat. Since you have not committed yourself one hundred percent to manifesting your miracle, the universe is not likely to respond.

The act of diving completely severs your connection to the land. Your security blanket evaporates; your safety net is gone. You can no longer turn and run back for protection. You have reached the point of no return where you will either sink or swim.

You might believe that you are the victim; you may think you have no choices. Your life is a rough uphill battle, and you live in fear, and everyone tells you it's impossible. I have come to tell you that there is always a way out, even if it takes time. Use your mind. Plan your personal escape. What move will you make next?

Think of it this way: if you stay on this destructive path you're on, you *will* eventually sink. You *will* fail. If you venture out, sure there's a risk, but your chances are much better, because you just might succeed. Plus, if you don't make it the first time, you can always keep trying. Each failure brings you one step closer to success. And if practice makes perfect, as they say, then you're actually guaranteed to win already, and you don't even know it. Don't do what works for you today. Consider your future, and do what's going to help you to survive in the long run.

If you're not convinced that change is necessary and you still doubt that you can achieve your dreams, we have some work to do.

What habits do you have that are keeping you from accomplishing your dreams? What hardship in your life has become intolerable to you? What challenge will you use as fuel for *your* miracle?

_____

_____

_____

_____

When and why did you develop this habit?

_____

_____

_____

_____

Recall a time when you wanted to help yourself or someone else and another person invalidated you for your attempts.

_____

_____

_____

_____

_____

_____

The first step in the formula is that you must have a strong desire to change. I'm not talking about a general discomfort with your life. What I'm referring to is that feeling that you cannot possibly go another day in this miserable state, and you decide, once and for all, there's no turning back now. Are you with me?

ADMITTING YOU HAVE A PROBLEM REALLY IS THE FIRST STEP

It sounds cliché, I know, but in order for you to start the changing and growing process, you've got to admit that you're in trouble. You've got to admit that you're looking for answers to your tough questions. You may not even know you have a serious problem. You might have excused your lethargy as boredom. At least one in twenty Americans are depressed; fear and anxiety have intensified as economic woes, natural disasters, and terrorism have increased.

Do you feel as if your life is in complete ruins? Maybe just one or two areas need improvement. One needn't be in serious danger to undergo transformation and growth, but oftentimes, crisis is a course correction mechanism that occurs when your life is not in sync with your purpose. Course corrections are actual steps taken to let go of the past and design a future that permits you to live the life you truly want to live.

Depressed or bored people do not usually make miracles, and even if they do, they assume that it's a fluke. Depression requires emotional, intellectual, and physical cleansing. If left untreated, it will destroy your entire life.

ARE YOU DEPRESSED?
SYMPTOMS OF DEPRESSION INCLUDE:

- Fatigue or loss of energy, sluggishness
- Mood swings
- Increased anxiety
- Feelings of worthlessness, despair, or excessive guilt
- Diminished ability to concentrate and focus
- Indecisiveness
- Overeating or loss of appetite
- Loss of interest in activities you used to enjoy
- Unwillingness to leave the house
- Feeling negative, tense, and angry
- Difficulty sleeping or sleeping too much
- Recurrent thoughts of death or specific plans to commit suicide

Depression is often linked to anger. Make a list of people you are angry with, including yourself.

_____

_____

_____

What are you upset about and why?

_____

_____

_____

_____

_____

_____

The natural laws that govern this physical universe contain two important components: cause and effect. Either you are causing something or you are the effect of something. It's just that simple. Examine any incident in your life, and you will find that you fell into one of the two categories.

People who are depressed have suffered by being at effect over and over again. They stay at home, no longer participating in life. They've had so many losses that they forget that they can change the tide. Feeling that they may never again be at cause, they start to sink into hopelessness and despair.

Think of it this way. Remember a time when you were playing a game, but you kept on loosing. It can be any game, really. What was your reaction to loosing the game over and over and over? Perhaps you've seen this in a child. What does the child do?

_____

_____

_____

_____

_____

_____

Well he gives up, of course. He stops playing the game. Life is nothing more than a big, big game. And those who are depressed have stopped playing.

The quickest way to turn it all around is to learn to be at cause again. It's not difficult. Whether you are depressed or not, answering the following questions will help you to move in a good direction.

What can you change today? Maybe it's something simple like moving your car or doing your hair. Perhaps it's something bigger. Whatever you have the ability to change, write it down.

_____

_____

_____

_____

_____

What do you have the ability to create?

_____

_____

_____

_____

What project could you do right now that would help you feel better?

_____

_____

_____

_____

If you could wave your miracle wand and enact one major (and seemingly impossible) change that would correct your life, what would it be?

_____

_____

_____

_____

_____

Your depression could be caused by imbalances related to your nutritional consumption. The link between your diet, your physical health, and your vitality has already been established. The cliché, 'you are what you eat' exists for a reason. Thus, getting in touch with your body's unique health needs will impact not only your physical health but your emotional stability as well.

Your nutritional needs are directly related to your blood type. There is no magical list that tells you what is good for and bad for all of us as one. But there are several lists that guide you towards healthy eating for your particular blood type. So for instance, yogurt, apples, and oranges may be healthy for one person and detrimental to another.

There are, of course, some things that we should all stay away from. Take coffee, for example. It is a great stimulant, but has a deleterious effect on your body. If it had a warning label, it would read, "warning ... drinking too much of this product may increase your chances of cancer in the stomach and pancreas, may cause ulcers, headaches, and mood swings. Worse, it is derived from the same organic family as cocaine and is highly addictive."

I have always had a problem with hypoglycemia related to

nutritional imbalances. If I don't eat properly, my blood sugar drops, and I break out into a cold, grey sweat, accompanied by faintness and sudden fatigue. Coffee aggravated the condition, creating an emotional roller coaster with exhaustion, mood swings, and panic attacks. I find that when I stop drinking coffee, my emotions stabilize, and I became calmer, happier, and less anxious.

Most of the time, I do not drink it anymore. However, occasionally the smell of a brewed cup of Colombian coffee will drive me insane, and I will have a cup, always telling myself that it's just this one cup. Caffeine is highly addictive, and within days I am back to drinking two to three cups a day. And inevitably, I am back on my emotional roller coaster until I stop drinking coffee again.

Remember to take good care of yourself, especially if you are depressed. We only have one body, so treat it well. Walk every day, whether you feel like it or not. Drink extra water and concentrate on natural foods, preferably organic and not loaded with preservatives and chemicals.

Opt for healthy alternatives as opposed to potentially dangerous medications. I admit that during my worst times, I turned to Paxil and Prozac, both strong anti-depressants. I was desperate for relief, and the drugs stabilized me. The medication gave me a bottom, a place I could land so I didn't feel like I was continually falling through. I didn't like taking the anti-depressants, because although they took the edge off my emotions, I felt distant. I stopped taking them as soon as I could, because I believe that the body can be healed from most ills through herbs, supplements, nutrition and the power of the mind.

If you are depressed, *do not* take psych drugs, and since you likely won't go back and read that statement again, allow me to reiterate. *Please beware* of the psychiatric scams out there to convince people that there is something wrong with them. All problems can be corrected by use of healthy alternatives. If you are taking these drugs, I urge you to wean yourself off of them as soon as possible.

Remember the Columbine Massacre? One of the two boys who created the blood bath was on anti-depressants. The drugs were supposed to make him feel better—not more hostile.

Don't take my word for it. Look on the back of most of the popular pills. There are now black box warnings that state that this drug could lead to sadness and depression.

I realize that this is a progressive idea, especially during a time when psychiatric drugs are rampant, but think about it. Drugs suppress symptoms, but they do not create balance in the body or mind. Even if you are *in favor of* anti-depressants, surely you've observed that psych drugs don't solve the actual problem; they simply act as a Band-Aid solution. They cover up the problem and create more. A drug is a drug. Whether you get it from your street dealer or your licensed professional, drugs are harmful. And being on any type of drugs makes it much more difficult to create miracles, large or small.

Your initial response to your rough life may be like mine—panic, grieving, and crying. I was the victim, bemoaning my losses to anyone who would listen. Following that path led me to depression, further loss, destitution, and near suicide. While you may need to experience those feelings for a short period of time, at some point, you must pick yourself up, brush off the excuses, and get on with life.

For those of you undergoing personal crisis, I lovingly guide you to look at the larger picture. Should you decide to follow this program, I can promise that the higher path you take will resolve the challenges. This is my wish for you: that you pick yourself up by your bootstraps and get on with your life. Turn your troubles into a wealth of opportunities by changing your attitude and building a new life.

It's all well and good for me to suggest you step outside yourself and look at the big picture. But when you are desperate, hungry, suicidal, and abused, you may not feel ready to hear what I'm saying. Your usual mode of expression might manifest in anxiety, worry, anger, depression, or illness. Faced with survival issues and loss, you could be experiencing a great deal of fear right now. If your self-confidence wavers because of tragic events, read on. If your life has been sent into a tailspin, stay with me. If you have any problems at all, large or small, this book is for you.

Inside every crisis is a potential bud of self-growth and change. As my nose-dive was happening, I heard a tiny voice that said, "you will lose it all, but you will rebuild and have more than you dreamed possible." That voice resides in you as well. Listen carefully. Although it may be muffled and hard to hear at times, it's there nonetheless. The same can be true for you if you allow good things into your life.

What good could come into your life right now?

_____

_____

_____

_____

_____

_____

_____

THE BIG PICTURE: SEEING YOUR LIFE IN PERSPECTIVE

I'm going to tell you a little secret about confronting issues. People avoid confronting pain and problems, because they think that if they don't look at it, they won't have to feel it, and everything will just be okay. Well that's just not the case. If you don't believe me, recall a time when you tried this. Did ignoring the issue solve your confusion or problem?

When you look at something, it gets handled. If you acknowledge a problem and confront it, the resolution automatically begins. That's the truth, and if you don't believe me, you're about to find out. When you confront a problem, you may feel a little discomfort at first, but trust me, the doors that it will unlock for you—the miracles that will happen in your life will feel *so* amazing, you won't even remember the fear of avoiding it. You may even feel silly for not doing this long ago.

Please don't skip the rest of this section. If you need to do it in doses, that's fine. Just do what you need to do to get it done. Also, don't glaze over it real quick and move on.

Answer the questions below as honestly as possible. Do not leave anything out, because you don't want to write it down. Get the dark clouds out of your system, for they weigh you down and create a heavier vibration. Doom and gloom, depression, and negative self-talk are dark emotions that block your success. Channel those feelings into hope.

I am upset because:

I am angry because:

I am frustrated because:

_____

I am happy because:

_____

I am excited because:

_____

I am content because:

_____

Your present life is the result of the decisions you made years ago. In fact, you designed your current state of being, whether you remember it or not. The fear and failure you are experiencing you will continue to attract unless you take charge now, and change your negative thinking immediately. *You must take responsibility for your life and the choices you've made.*

As rough as this sounds, it's essential, and avoiding or brushing over it is the equivalent to pretending like you're not standing in quicksand when you are. Misplaced blame is a pit, and while you may think it makes you feel better to avoid responsibility, this is the very thing that's holding you back from progressing.

Taking responsibility for your life is a catch-22 situation. You avoid doing it, because you think it will make you feel worse about the mistakes you made. So it's uncomfortable to own up to the problems you caused, but just as soon as you do, you have wonderful revelations and a whole new world opens up to you. Know the saying, "the truth will set you free"? Nothing could be more applicable here.

And let's be honest. You didn't get to this terrible place by doing charity work. If you want to activate miracles, you've got to get real before you can move on to the next step.

It's time to rebuild your life, harness your challenges, and alter your course. By taking the time to view your life in perspective, and by creating a large picture first, you will have the power to enable miracles.

This is a process I like to do when I need to step outside myself to see what is really going on. Close your eyes, and take a deep breath. Imagine you are outside the planet, peering at Earth, and then look in the direction of your home. See your building as it draws you closer and closer to it.

As you descend gently towards your home, pay attention to the exterior qualities. Note if it is pleasing or not. Is it beautiful and elegant and peaceful? Is it shabby, impoverished, or turbulent? Is it beautiful yet lonely and cold? Walk around the house and up to the front door, taking mental notes of what you see around you. The idea is to objectively observe your life from an outsider's point of view.

Walk into this home and peer into nooks and crannies as you try to understand the nature of the being living here. Is the kitchen inviting and homey? Is it the heart of the household? What type of person lives here? Are there flowers and pets? Do you feel loving, cozy, and calm feelings? Or do you feel stress in the air speckled with chaotic discomfort? Glide inside your bedroom. See the sleeping figure of you lying in your bed. What do you feel about this person? What type of person lies before you?

When you're ready, open your eyes, and write down your impressions of yourself, your surroundings, and the general feelings you experienced. The visualization process should allow you to see yourself from a different perspective, a paradigm shift that will help give you clarity as to why these situations occur in your life and how this time you can handle them differently.

It is normal to experience anger, fear, anxiety, or sorrow. Rather than minimizing these feelings, write them down. Admit you are emotional, and allow time to grieve—but also allow yourself to acknowledge the truth of what is wrong, and then move on.

_____

_____

_____

_____

_____

_____

_____

_____

Look around your home. Notice the areas that need improvement. Where you have been lying to yourself, lying to others, procrastinating, making excuses, and denying your own culpability?

If you were a stranger, would you want to live in this home? How does your environment make you feel? Are you proud of your home, or are there messes everywhere? Write down your impressions. Your home reflects the vibration you send to the world.

_____
_____
_____
_____

Did you like some of what you saw? What things would you keep as they are, if given the opportunity to change the scene? What is right with your world? What is working for you? What miracles are already present?

_____
_____
_____
_____

Realistically assess your current situation. List every worst-fear scenario that you have. Remember, confronting is the only way to overcome these fears, and knowledge is power. By doing these writing exercises, you will begin to learn valuable lessons about yourself.

My worst fears, including the ones I don't admit to myself, are:

_____
_____
_____
_____

Imagine that your life just gets worse and worse. What is the most horrible thing that could happen to you right now?

_____
_____

_____

_____

_____

What good could come from that crisis you imagined?

_____

_____

_____

_____

What is it that makes you feel safe, and where do you turn for help? Also, is the person or place or thing you're clinging to in times of distress, healthy for you?

_____

_____

_____

_____

_____

What are you running from?

_____

_____

_____

_____

What are you hiding from yourself, and why?

_____

_____

_____

What did you see that needs improvement? List everything that is out of harmony.

_____

_____

_____

_____

Did you have any realizations?

_____

_____

_____

_____

CONFESSIONAL

For this next section, you're really going to focus on owning up to the mistakes you've made. This essential part of examining your life will lead to miracles beyond your wildest imagination.

As you write down the names of people, mentally speak with them, and tell them that you are sorry for any pain you created in their lives. Explain to them that you did not know any better but that you're now making a concerted effort to get well. Ask them to forgive you, and then, most important, forgive yourself. Remind yourself that you are a Miracle Maker in training (you are just not perfect yet.) You don't have to actually confront these people for this exercise to work. You just need to face your personal words and actions—with honesty.

In what areas of your life could you improve? Consider the following areas: family, health, career, financial, spiritual, interpersonal relationships, and life style decisions.

_____
_____
_____
_____
_____
_____
_____
_____

In what areas of your life are you neglecting your personal ethics?

_____
_____
_____
_____
_____

What have you promised and failed to perform?

_____
_____
_____
_____
_____

Whom have you hurt accidentally or intentionally?

_____
_____
_____
_____

Why did I create this negativity in my life and the lives of others?

_____

_____

_____

_____

How do I sabotage myself and create resistance? How am I standing in my own way?

_____

_____

_____

_____

How does this fit into the perspective of what I truly want?

_____

_____

_____

_____

What is the lesson I am learning now?

_____

_____

_____

_____

And most important, how can I turn this all around and make it into something positive?

_____

_____

_____

_____

Congratulations! You're on the road to success. The real journey has just begun.

Your next step is to make an effort to stop doing these not-so good things that you do. Now that you have confronted the bad, you can forget about it. No longer focus on the negative. It's all bright and sunny days from here on. Focus only on the good and positive.

I challenge myself daily to be sensitive to the needs of everyone around me, including my pets. It's not easy to keep track of, but it makes a huge difference. If you make attempts at getting better and then you fail, forgive yourself of not being perfect, and then get right back up and keep trying. By just making those attempts, you and everyone around you will notice a difference. Beating yourself up is not a good trait, so just go ahead and put yourself off the hook. It won't help you and has no place in the new you.

Evil phrases include: "I can't" and "I shouldn't have" and "it's all _____'s fault" These words will take hold of your spirit and slow you down. When you say these things to yourself or others, you cringe, because you are forced to retreat within for security and safety. Treat yourself and others with tender, loving kindness. Nurture your inner child, and create an aura of peace and harmony. Send out positive thoughts, and you, in kind, will receive the benefit. Who are you, anyway? The friend or the enemy? As a general rule, if you wouldn't want someone to say it to you, don't say it to yourself.

Now. Take a deep breath and relax. The next chapter deals with lighter subjects that will help progress your future to a better place. Remember, the more good you put out, the more positive you'll attract inward.

You are responsible for the life you are living.
You have within, the potential to redesign your life.
It is possible to create a new future.
Activate your miracle magnet and attract happiness.

PART TWO

HOW to MAKE MIRACLES

CHAPTER FOUR

DISCOVERING YOUR LIFE'S PURPOSE

So you've struggled through the difficult parts. Now it's time to get to the bottom of this. *Why* are you here?

This path requires courage, and I can't do it for you. To hear your own drummer, requires that others may find you distant or call you strange. But if you don't follow your own path, you are compromising yourself. You must make your own decisions and answer to your higher calling.

You start by visualizing and writing down what you want. Allow yourself to dream about the possibilities. Use fanciful words like, "what if I could or would do that?" Then upgrade your thinking to, "I can do that." Finally, make that leap and say to yourself, "I will do that." Always affirm, "I am a magnet for miracles. I am a magnet for wealth. I am miracle magnet."

Your inner dream might be secreted in a locked box, hidden

beneath layers of invalidation where you cannot find it, but it is within you, nonetheless. Listen to the fragments or remnants of dreams that reside in the back of your consciousness. No matter how deep you bury your truth, you will always hear its faint call and echoes. There is no running from it, because it is you who knows the truth.

Close your eyes, and ask yourself, "What am I here to do? What am I here to accomplish?" Oftentimes, you already have the answer, or you hear it immediately, like a soft whisper in the back of your mind. Frequently, this is the voice you negate or ignore by stopping yourselves and saying, "This is too bold and too brave. I can't do that." You've got to learn to trust yourself. What if Edison had given up after 999 attempts to create the light bulb? You might be reading this book by a burning candle!

You were meant to have a fulfilling and prosperous life, but at some point, you veered from the path. You ventured down another way, but today's the day that you get back on track and find your true calling. Imagine it this way. In your mind, see a corridor with two doors. Behind door A, is the life you dream about, the fulfilling, purposeful, positive, miraculous existence where dreams come true for you.

Behind door B, is the mundane, routine, non-fulfilling world you have found yourself in, where you feel lack, bored, anxious or unfulfilled. By believing in your own ability to make miracles, you can shift from behind door B, to door A and get on track. You were born with a unique set of challenges and a "raison d'etre." Isn't it about time you rediscover your potential?

REDISCOVER THE BEAUTY OF YOU

In a scene from Alice and Wonderland, the Caterpillar asks Alice, "who are *you*?" Alice responds, "I - I hardly know, sir, just at present - at least I know who I was when I got up this morning, but I think I must have been changed several times since then."

"What do you mean by that?" asked the annoyed Caterpillar.

"I can't explain myself, I'm afraid, sir," said Alice, "because I am not myself, you see."

"I don't see," said the Caterpillar.

If you don't know who you are, then you won't have the good fortune to share your greatest gifts with others. Do the following exercises to learn more about yourself.

What brings you joy?

_____

_____

_____

_____

_____

Make a list of all the things you love about your life and yourself.

_____

_____

_____

_____

_____

Make a list of things you love but are not yet a part of your life.

_____

_____

_____

_____

_____

List your outstanding qualities as a human being. In what areas do you excel?

_____

_____

_____

_____

_____

In what areas do you *want to* excel?

_____

_____

_____

_____

_____

Why do others want to be around you? This is not the time to be modest. Sing your praises. Imagine you are listening to one of your best friend's description of you to another. What would they say about you? Be truthful.

_____

_____

_____

_____

Are you starting to notice any patterns or consistencies? If so, what has been a common theme throughout all of your answers?

_____

_____

_____

_____

_____

NOTHING IS IMPOSSIBLE IN DAMANHUR

Words are *so* important to your success. When I was in the Federation of Damanhur, located in Northern Italy, I interviewed the founder of the community.

In 1975, Oberto Airaudi, now known as Falco, began to build an underground temple as well as a magical mystery school. This internationally renowned center for spiritual research, located in the foothills of northern Italy, is an amazing community with over 800 citizens. It has its own Constitution, currency, political structure, schools, 100 businesses, organic farms, winery, and a daily newspaper.

The community began with two-dozen citizens with a vision. They dreamed of a society based on optimism and the idea that human beings can be the masters of their own destiny and fulfill their individual potential. Each citizen I met reaffirmed the principles that they followed their individual callings, within the framework of a community that encourages this as part of the collective mission.

Falco matter of factly informed me that the word "impossible" has been banned from their vocabulary. We were discussing the fact that building the temples seemed an almost impossible task. But not to Damanhurians, he informed me with a twinkle in his eye. Just as in Camelot, nothing is impossible in Damanhur.

What is most amazing about Damanhur is the Underground Temples of Humankind, carved by hand from rock by these citizens. The temple tells the story of the history of mankind through the use of ancient artistic techniques such as mosaics in glass and stone, sculptures, and marble. Many people have described these temples as the eighth wonder of the world. Falco and ten other Damanhurians picked up hammers and chisels, shovels, and picks and began to dig the temple. They worked practically non-stop and dug a tunnel into the side of the mountain. The temple measures 70 meters from the highest to the lowest point and is the equivalent of an eleven-story building. There are six different levels connected by hundreds of meters of corridors. Sounds like an "impossible" feat, now doesn't it?

Basically, it was one man's vision that drew together the community and created the vision of the temples. Even though it looked to be an impossible, he refused to accept that. His motto is that if it is deemed impossible, then they can do it.

This exemplifies the power of words. While others say "can't," Falco and his peers said, "watch us." Like Falco, you are successful to the degree that you decide you are.

Watch what you tell yourself on a minute-by-minute basis. What messages are you sending yourself? Are you repeating negative thoughts throughout the day, and if so, what are they?

_____

_____

_____

_____

There is never an excuse to use foul language to yourself or anyone else. This negativity will breed more indecision. The thoughts you tell yourself govern your very being with results following accordingly.

To show you what I mean, play a little game called the "muscle test." Grab two friends. Two evenly matched people will arm wrestle, and the third person will send out negative energy to one person in the competition. He doesn't have to stand there cursing and yelling. He just needs to think negative thoughts such as "you fail, you loose, you die." Observe who wins. Do it again with the third person sending negative energy to the opposite person. Next, ask them to send out positive thoughts, and note the results.

The mistake you make is that you don't remember or recognize that the space around you, all that stuff you think is empty, is actually filled with invisible matter. Some of this matter is in the form of our messages and thoughts. Think positive thoughts and waves of beautiful molecules emanate from you. They spread the good around, inoculating the less fortunate cells. Attach negative thoughts around you and attract negative energies like bees to honey.

> *You can do it*
> *if you believe you can!*
> —NAPOLEON HILL

The great Albert Einstein once said, "There are two ways to live your life. One is as though nothing is a miracle, the other is as though everything is a miracle." Frankly, I prefer to live as if everything were a miracle. Because funny enough, the more I live my life as if it were a miracle, the more miraculous my life becomes.

Let's take this a step further. Just like Einstein, I believe you have two choices in your approach to life. You can choose an ordinary, mundane existence, or you can choose a higher calling, leading you to a miraculous way of living. Only you can decide where you are headed.

GOOD VIBRATIONS

Miracles happen all the time, everyday, to every type of person, but when you fail to recognize them as miracles, you loose your powers. There is a way that you can visualize, practice for, and prepare to create miracles. All you have to do is raise your vibration.

The air around us is filled with atoms and sub-atoms, particles, electrons, thought waves, sound waves, light waves, angel waves ... you name it, and it is there. This is not empty space. Think of your thoughts as an order or request that you are sending directly out into the universe, which sends you back exactly what you asked for. A negative thought clings to your aura or energy field for days, looking like bags of black hanging on you. At least, that's how it makes you feel—heavy and weighed down, a blackened mood.

To catch your miracle wave and allow this shift into your life, you must raise your vibration to a higher frequency. Love, peace, happiness, and laughter, shift your energy noticeably. Certain people make you feel healthier and happier just to be around. They leave you feeling changed. Other people give off negative vibes and can leave you feeling drained.

Look at vibration this way ... we are like antennas with an

electromagnetic field. The more finely tuned and sensitive our antennas, the higher the frequency will resonate back. Imagine sending your antenna high up into the ethers—into space—to attract a "heavenly" charge. The higher you can raise your antenna, the greater the positive charge of joy, happiness, and all the good feelings.

Here is a great meditation exercise you can do to raise your vibration. The miracle wand is a tool we sell at www.miraclemakersclub.com. Its purpose is to cleanse your personal space and attract positive energy from the physical universe.

If you don't have one, pretend, but the idea is to physically do this so that you can visualize the process. Raise your wand up towards the sky with your eyes closed. Increase your vibration by using the miracle wand as a conduit of positive electro magnet waves of energy that will flow through. By doing this, you become a magnet for these particles of energy that bring you exactly what you are asking for.

As you raise your wand, verbalize what you want. You can say, "I am a magnet for miracles. I am raising my vibration to attract miracles. The higher my vibration, the more miracles I attract. My life is guided, intuitive, holistic and prosperous." Feel free to say it however it best fits your life and needs. You can say anything or ask for anything, so long as it's positive.

Every obstacle, obstruction, and challenge, tests your potential and makes you stronger until you hear the call and awaken. The miracle wand is a tool to remind you that you are a Miracle Maker. When you find yourself in challenging situations, touch the wand in your back pocket to remind you of who you are.

Believing in miracles takes faith, confidence, and a willingness to try something new, instead of living in the same old, same old. A miraculous moment in time is a paradigm shift, resulting in things suddenly going your way. When I make the right decision, my heart literally sings, and I hear a whistling inside. When I am in the midst of a miracle, my entire face smiles wide, and my chest stretches with happiness and pure joy.

While creating your miracles, you're living your highest of selves. You're not guided by a bland, pious altruism but by true excitement, passion and intuition. This is your core, the voice that would walk a million miles just to taste from the cup of spiritual fulfillment and have a life with meaning. This is your soul essence expressing itself on the planet. I believe that when a person is living their true, inner purpose, that is a miracle, especially since our culture is materialistic based, not mission based.

WHAT IS YOUR MISSION STATEMENT?

Everyone has a purpose on this planet—a mission that's his or hers alone. Purposes come in all shapes, sizes, and forms. I have a little secret to share about the mission statement, and this might make it a little easier on you while trying to figure out your own purpose. The entire race of humankind has a common mission, and that mission is to help. It's just that simple. We are all here to help. Help ourselves; help our neighbors; help humankind; we're here to help someone or something.

Within that larger purpose, each individual has a specific path. Your mission might be to nurture and support your family, or it might be to support others by cleaning and organizing their home. Your mission might be to bring joy through music or to deliver flowers to the sad. Every person, from the housekeeper and the garbage man to the doctor and the astronaut, plays an important role in the grand scheme of life.

Do you know your mission statement? Perhaps you think you do, but you need to hone it somewhat. I recommend writing it down. Use your notes from the earlier chapters in this book to guide you. It could take you one paragraph or ten. It doesn't matter. Just write and write and write. Even if you already *know for certain* what it is, just write.

_____

_____

_____

_____

_____

_____

_____

_____

_____

_____

_____

_____

_____

_____

_____

_____

_____

_____

_____

_____

When you discover that purpose, life plans become clear, and you can live your life with intention, motivation and fulfillment. That is the key to health, wealth, and happiness. But then, some of you already know for a fact why you're here, and to you, I ask, "are you living that purpose every day?"

Take me. I knew I was here to heal and inspire millions. I assumed that one day in the future, once my plan was working, I would finally live my fantasy life. Once things were perfect, *then* I would become the woman I really was meant to be. In my fantasy, I am a future author. I knew that my purpose was to help, and someday, I would surely do that.

But I was confused, you see? My life wasn't changing itself for me, as I'd hoped. Waiting for this grandiose scenario got me nowhere. I had been inadequate for the task assigned to me. My depression grew deeper since I had failed in my mission. Just knowing your purpose is not enough. You've got to do something about it today.

ONE MORNING A THUNDERBOLT STRUCK; I finally got it. I was supposed to be living my purpose on a daily basis, now, not waiting for the future. This cognition forced me to confront my fears of failure. I was afraid that if I believed in myself, I would lose the dream altogether. If I tried to follow this calling and I failed, I would be crushed. I created many excuses until one day, I could no longer pretend.

Gregg Levoy, author of *Callings: Finding and Following an Authentic Life*, says that "Saying yes to the call tends to place you on a path that half of yourself thinks doesn't make a bit of sense, but the other half knows your life won't make sense without." He believes that by following our deepest calling, we are filled with both "exhilaration and terror". You want to listen to the call, but your negative self talk seeds fear, timidity, confusion, doubt, and anxiety. It's easier (just for today) to remain stuck, unhappy, and tied to what you know. But what about tomorrow and next year?

Once I said, "My life can't get worse than this. Something's gotta give," I discovered new ideas and new projects. My inner creative genius awoke and imagined new ways to accomplish my dream. I began to focus on what I could do, and I suddenly developed clarity. I once again had direction. It was as if I were magically being guided by my intuitive voice to go in the right direction. Once I stopped saying, "no" and started saying, "yes," an entire new life opened up to me.

The beauty is you don't have to know exactly how you are going to accomplish all of your goals. You just have to believe in yourself enough to try. You must walk each step that guides you along your path to where you are going. The destination becomes clearer as you catch your miracle wave, hear your calling and develop your passion.

Ideally, you'll just decide you can do something and then go do it. You'll just postulate it. If you can't just believe in yourself in order to make your dreams come true, act *as if* you believe, and take the steps, as if it were actually going to lead you to the results you want. Do whatever you need to do to start (or continue) living your life on purpose.

For me to get started making my dream a reality, I had to get busy. After all, this club wasn't going to get up and make itself. I went to the county records and applied for a business license. I added a separate phone line. I developed a business plan, reorganized my files, and designed my marketing materials. I sent out e-mails and promotional materials to hundreds of women's organizations, job loss groups, churches, and foundations offering my speaking services. I was ready to start sharing my story. I wrote and self published the *Survival Kit*, and I'm following it up with this book.

Today, as I complete this manuscript, I realize that I am living my destiny. I am in my future, because that's what I created. I am now an author, speaker, and consultant who lives quietly but passionately with her two children in a beautiful house with a pool and a sports court—exactly as we fantasized it. And you can do this too.

What could you start doing today for these dreams to come true?

_____

_____

_____

_____

_____

_____

_____

_____

_____

_____

_____

Once I did it, I was ready to spread the good word. One of my friends is involved in an abusive relationship and lives in Section 8 (or low income) housing. She currently works as a housekeeper, yet as a young woman she traveled around the world and lived a cultured, sophisticated artistic life. In her cell membranes, she has the memory of her wealth and prosperity, but now she cannot access those feelings of joy. Because she's been in this relationship, her confidence and will to live has eroded. Even allowing herself to fantasize a better life, she believes, is impossible for her, because she has lost hope and no longer feels deserving. She informed me the other day that she couldn't imagine herself in any other scenario than what she has now. She couldn't see herself having a more comfortable life style, because her self-esteem is diminished, and she felt too small and inadequate to dream larger. Her life was the equivalent to what she knew it would be. Nothing more. It saddens me to remind you, dear reader, that what you think and what you expect, is what you see and what you get. That's why it is important not to lose your dreams.

Now for this part, go ahead and get out all of those negative thoughts. Why are you *not* living your purpose? What are your obstacles?

Trust in one thing—you would not have these callings unless you were destined to be and do those things. This is not the time to put others first and adjust your thinking to please or satisfy someone else. This is *your* life path and *your* life mission. Are you really going to believe that another person knows what's best for you? Ask yourself: is that person who discouraged you living *their* life dreams?

One of my good friends was inspired to make a transformational shift in her life. The steps we had just designed would take her from scarcity to prosperity in 120 days or less. She had created the journey to her dreams. She left my presence, bold and determined. I warned her to remain silent regarding her new steps unless she was with a fellow Miracle Maker. She agreed, but she shared her vision with her best friend who basically shot her down. She called that night in a panic, fearing that her new plans were now impossible.

Her best friend was what I call a dream buster. This type of person doesn't want to support you in being all that you can. They want to bust your bubble. They tell you, convincingly, "you won't ever make it." Because they are your "friends", you unwillingly accept what they tell you about yourself. You start to believe it for yourself, and boom, the miracle wave has passed you over.

"But," you might say, "They could know what they're talking about. They're older than me and must be more wise than me." And I say to you, that's good, but what's your point? Only you know what is right for you. Age is irrelevant. You won't know what is going to work and what is going to fail until you give it a try and observe for yourself.

You are unlimited; there is no stopping you. Let your wildest imagination out of the box and experience your vast potential. The universe has no limits. It is endless and boundless. That is why so few of us sleep outside under the stars. Humans prefer walls and ceilings to protect them from the outer elements, cutting us from our connection with the immensity of the galaxy. The bad news is these walls can close us in and keep us small. Stop closing the door on your success.

Your conscious commitment to creating miracles increases as you overcome obstacles. By focusing on the miraculous possibilities, you attract the right people to assist you. I call these people miracle allies. These people can guide you, and you can help them. They will lift you up and strengthen you. They will validate that you need to follow that voice in your mind.

Last week, one of my girlfriends was honored by the local fair housing association. She had courageously lifted herself from poverty and got her college degree. After her speech, one person came up and gave her the names of people in the area that would give her the work she was seeking. That's a miracle ally.

A miracle buddy is another being who believes in master-minding and is recreating their life. They are following their intuitive calling and designing a life that supports them in doing this. Share your plans and your commitments with your buddy on a daily or weekly basis or whatever it takes to keep you both on track. Outline the action steps, and be specific. Review your goals and accomplishments, and brainstorm imaginative ways to reach your dreams. Become a cheering squad for your comrade on your journey to success. Inspire each other onward and upward.

Besides this one ally, surround yourself with positive people. Look for individuals fulfilling their potential. Let them be your role models, and share your success stories. Find out how others have traveled on this journey before you. Read the stories of famous leaders and mentors. Find your heroes and study them. Stop wasting time with time wasters and people who depress you or aren't living up to their potential.

Brainstorm with your miracle buddies how you will live when you are fabulously wealthy and living the life of your dreams. Where will you live? How will you decorate? What will you do for fun? Make it a Miracle Making game and have fun. Trips to Tahiti and Brazil, why not? Who said you are here to sacrifice and have a miserable life. You create your misery, now go and create joy!

If you follow the exercises in this book, there will come a time when things magically seem to click and life just goes your way. The right people enter into your life. Special and often unexplainable things may start occur. Your inner voice will be louder and more active than ever before, and you will sense that you have an important future. Those moments give you hope and build confidence.

Who has supported you, been there for you and helped you through rough times? Who has never doubted that you have amazing potential?

My miracle buddies are:

_____

_____

_____

My dream busters are:

_____

_____

_____

Who told you that you couldn't have a prosperous, fulfilling life? Who convinced you that you couldn't follow this life path? Who insisted you conform and follow the rules? How old were you when you stopped dreaming? Was there someone in your childhood who insisted that you change your life's coarse?

_____

_____

_____

_____

_____

Believe in yourself. If you don't have faith
that you can do it, who will?

Once you recognize your life's theme, the mission and quest
you have chosen, your life will finally begin. That's when you'll
transform the depression into passion to achieve your dreams.

JOAN'S STATEMENT OF PURPOSE:

My purpose is to activate and inspire millions of people to
become the makers of millions of miracles throughout our
planet. I am committed to making a difference in people's lives
by supporting them to achieve their dreams!

A life without purpose
is a sad life indeed!
Not to mention boring, mediocre,
and uneventful.
Why would you bother?
Your thoughts govern
your life; think positive thoughts.
Allow yourself to
dream big.
Dream your unlimited future!

CHAPTER FIVE

CREATING A PERSONAL
PLAN THAT WORKS

ONE OF THE FIRST RULES of manifesting miracles is to rid your life of clutter. If you're seriously going to make changes, the time has come to completely reorganize everything. By keeping a clean home, you can accomplish more mentally. What do you have around your home that needs to be organized?

March resolutely into your closet and make a pile of things that you do not need. Either sell it at a yard sale, give it away to friends, or donate it to charity. Get rid of clothes that do not fit, looks bad on, or is associated with bad memories. I just finally threw out favorite pajamas, because every time I looked at them, the unwanted memory of my miracle buster comes to mind. And he is the last person I want to think about now as I go forward. If you're keeping clothing just because you think you should, go ahead and give it away. Out with the old. The universe loves a vacuum and will do all it can to replenish it.

During this process of de-cluttering, don't ask yourself if you like it or not. Of coarse you like it. Either you bought it (which means you like it), or someone gave it to you. And if you kept it for this long, you must like it. Look at each item with an individual eye and ask if you *use* it. Have you used it in the last few months? If the answer is no, no matter how reluctant, put it in the "out" pile.

Do this to all your closets. It doesn't matter if you have few possessions as long as they serve you well and make you feel good. Eating from broken plates is bad for your self -esteem. By clearing out your clutter, you will be making room for prosperity. Throw out the broken and decide to get something new. Even if you throw out two thirds of your stuff, this activity will serve you well.

New possessions and clothing will come to you.

CHECK LIST:

- Clean and reorganize your closets and drawers
- Get rid of clothing you have not worn for over a year
- Get rid of the boxes of stuff you have never unpacked
- Organize your computer, your desk, and your files
- Catch up on correspondence and return phone calls
- Pay your bills
- Finish other miscellaneous projects that you have been meaning to do.

Project completion signals to the universe that you are ready to move on to the next task—miracle making. Each time you finish a cycle of action, you indicate that your commitment to moving forward is now one hundred percent.

TASKS I NEED TO COMPLETE:

_____anticipated completion date_____

_____anticipated completion date_____

_____anticipated completion date_____

_____anticipated completion date_____

_____anticipated completion date_____

_____anticipated completion date_____

_____anticipated completion date_____

_____anticipated completion date_____

TAKING CARE OF NUMBER ONE

In the midst of crisis, health can go by the way side. When I was down and out, I stopped taking care of my body physically and mentally. A friend pointed out that I needed to nurture and feed myself first. "Get back to basics," she insisted, "take care of yourself, build your foundation, and eat foods that actually nourish your body. Once you get your physical vitality back on track, you will be able to focus on rebuilding your life."

Without good health, you cannot implement miracles properly. Your body must be tuned up a notch so that your vibration will shift. The fastest way to brew your miracles is to cleanse your body of toxins. You are what you eat. A diet consisting of fast foods and highly processed foods can slow you down. You'll become too sluggish to catch your miracle wave.

The purpose of eating is to nurture the body and provide us with the building blocks to properly function. We require healthy foods to support the vitality and sustenance required to follow our mission and life plan. By changing your diet, you will begin to feel significantly healthier, and you will be filled with the energy to focus on your goals. Eating better results in your body having enhanced vitality. Your natural enthusiasm and zest for life returns and spins you off into the miracle wave.

- Bless your food prior to eating and ask that it nourish your body, mind, and spirit. Give thanks and gratitude for the bounty provided. Each food has a life force that matches a similar frequency within your body. Even the process of eating can activate harmony and peace throughout your inner body or disharmony as well.

- Eat small, frequent meals throughout the day. This will release natural sugar into your bloodstream throughout the day, keeping your energy balanced and normal.

- Avoid sugar, candy, and other unhealthy snack foods.

Substitute raw vegetables and fruits like carrots, celery, apples, and mangos.

- Go organic. Eliminate foods grown with pesticides and antibiotics.

- Drink 64 ounces of purified water daily. (That's eight glasses.) Begin your day with a glass of warm water with a half squeezed lemon to wake your liver and flush toxins from your system.

- Cut out coffee and sodas.

- If you are a smoker, now is the time to quit. You most likely know you need to, so perhaps this won't seem so harsh. If you stop smoking, substitute the urge to pick up a cigarette by eating crunchy vegetables or holding a pencil.

- Visit a chiropractor several times a month for preventive and wellness health care. Tune up your nervous system and have your body function at one hundred percent. Work with alternative health care providers to devise a system that keeps you health.

- Try taking SAM-e (S-Adenosyl-methionine). It was discovered in Italy in 1952 and used throughout Europe for twenty years as a mood enhancer for people with depression. Healthy people produce enough SAM-e, while depressed people have impaired production. Recent studies conducted by the Health and

Human Services Agency found it was also effective for liver disease and relieving joint pain. Do your own research on this to make sure that it's right for you, and read the directions carefully before use.

- Drink fresh wheatgrass juice. It is detoxifying and contains about 30 enzymes and one ounce of wheatgrass juice contains the vitamin and mineral equivalent of 2 lbs. of fresh vegetables.

- B vitamins and B complex can help with deficiencies, which result in mood swings, anxiety, stress, and irritability.

- Bach flower remedies are taken for individual emotional mood shifts such as worry, apprehension, anxiety, fear, irritability, and depression. There are thirty-eight remedies, and they have no side effects or unpleasant reactions.

- Herbs such as Skullcap, Oats, Vervain, and Wood Betony relieve stress. For anxiety and tension, try a tea of equal parts of skullcap and valerian. Other useful herbs include Siberian Ginseng, Licorice, Chamomile, and Nettles.

- Omega-3 fish oils. This completely cured my psoriasis, but it's also taken to fight off depression and enhance your immune system.

- Exercise plays an important role. Walk every morning, jog, go to the gym, do yoga, dance, swim, or work out. Walking two miles in the morning is a great way to wake up and relax.

I am probably the laziest person on the planet. I have had to motivate myself to walk the dog so that we can exercise. I joined a gym but refused to take the time to go. My son begs me to play basketball, and I find excuses. This was acceptable until I recently found my body fatigued, pale, and not up to the demands I was placing upon myself. I began experiencing anxiety and severe leg cramps, and I no longer awoke with enthusiasm. Thank goodness I discovered yoga as a way to move my body in a peaceful and harmonious manner.

The Chinese system of healing correlates symptoms with emotions. For example, lower back pain is associated with feeling sorry for yourself, and anger symbolizes not getting your needs met, not being taken care of, or worries about money and the lack of money. Oftentimes when I treated patients as a chiropractor, the healing wouldn't start until the underlying emotional components were acknowledged and dealt with. Neck pain and upper back pain is associated with stressing out about multiple problems and carrying the world on your shoulders, just like the mythological figure, Atlas. Knee problems stem from being afraid to stand on your own two feet. You get the idea.

In Louise Hays' book, *Heal Your Body*, she links specific health problems with its related feelings. Take for example bladder problems or urinary tract infections. According to Hays, the corresponding emotion is "anxiety, holding on to old ideas, fear of letting go, being pissed off." She suggests the affirmation, " I comfortably and easily release the old and welcome the new in my life. I am safe." For headaches, she suggests that you might be invalidating the self. Her remedy for curing headaches is for you to affirm, " I love and approve of myself. I see myself and what I do with eyes of love. I am safe."

Jose Silva, founder of Silva Mind Control, developed a technique to use your mind to heal your body. He found that by learning to go into alpha, a state of meditation, you can give your body healing suggestions to function properly and heal yourself. You can do this type of reprogramming by using mental images of what you want for yourself and your body. According to Jose Silva in his book, *You The Healer*, "Our bodies are equipped for self healing. We interfere with this natural process by reacting to events with worry and stress. We can withdraw this interference by responding to external events with relaxed reactions. We can also harness a healing energy by conceiving positive mental pictures and positive mentally verbalized instructions"

It all goes back to positive visualizations.

Yesterday I was watching my son Anton shoot hoops. He used to get about fifty to seventy-five percent of his free throws when playing basketball. But just recently he fractured his right clavicle. It had just healed, but his strength or style must not have been right on the mark, because only two out of ten got in the basket. I suggested he visualize himself in position to do the shot, exactly as he does it, and see it going directly into the hoop. He opened his eyes and landed eight straight free throws!

There is a direct correlation between the choices you make and the health issues you have.

Once your home, your car, your body and your life are clean, organized and energetic, your miracles will start to fall into place, and you are prepared to begin your new life.

YOU ARE WHAT YOU WEAR

Even if you're going jogging in the park, why not throw on a cute jogging suit? As I mentioned earlier, I was to the point of wearing whatever clothes I could get my hands on. This is not the way to go. Ragged old sweats aren't designed with high fashion in mind; they are built for comfort. But how comfortable can you be when you don't feel good on the inside?

My current dress code reflects my present state of mind. Things are different now. I occasionally let myself shop for new and exciting looks. I wear clothing that I have bought on my travels, a black skirt with frills and a matching black top. I scrunch up my hair so it is curly, and guess what? It just so happens that I think I look drop dead gorgeous. That's really all that matters. When you put it on, how do you feel? If you don't feel good about yourself, go ahead and take it off.

While in Italy, I bought cute tops from the outdoor farmers market. On hot days, with a mini skirt or capri pants, I think my clothes make me look downright delectable.

I love wearing clothing that I have bought in various countries, because when I dress, it reminds me of the trip and all of the fabulous memories there.

You don't have to go jet setting across the world to compile your wardrobe. Each person is different. It doesn't have to cost a fortune either. Just make wise choices. Who cares if it comes from Target so long as it makes you feel pretty while wearing it.

YOUR MIRACLE MAKING JOURNAL

Try this. For the next thirty days, commit to your journal. Here is where you will list your miracles as they happen including the little idiosyncrasies, curious patterns, and coincidences. Record your dreams, hopes, and affirmations. Finally, record your commitments to yourself and others. Add to the Miracle Making journal daily, and before you know it, you will attract an entire new set of life circumstances.

You can add pictures from magazines and photos you've taken to give yourself an extra boost. If you walk down the street and see a house that looks just like the one in your dreams, take pictures of it, or draw it for your notebook. Refer to this journal frequently when you require motivation or you don't know if you can survive one more day. Keep a section for action steps, where you chart your progress towards your goals.

Carry your Miracle Making notebook with you at all times, for you never know when inspiration will strike. I wrote the beginning of my very first paid article while driving over the Golden Gate Bridge in a fierce rainstorm. Do not lose your great ideas. Promise yourself that you will not judge the results. This is your space where you are free to visualize and plan your future.

Using your personal mission statement, write a motto, and say it to yourself daily. Continue to do this exercise until you have reached clarity. If you say it out loud and doubt creeps in, you haven't said it enough. Write it on several index cards, and carry your motto with you everywhere you go. Place one on your desk, one in your room, and another one in the bathroom. Organize your life in a way that you can't help but visualize your purpose. You can do this mental exercise with other things you want to accomplish as well.

The purpose of your dream journal is to write it down and make it known to yourself. Taking the time to write it out, I've found, is a little more effective than just thinking about it.

Now that you have made it clear to yourself and the universe, just what it is that you need and want, it's a good idea to visualize it over and over. I took my first goal-setting seminar in 1980 when I arrived in San Francisco as a new starving graduate of chiropractic college. I wasn't sure if writing down goals worked, but I was willing to test it. My number one goal was to find a place to live overlooking the San Francisco Bay—rent-free. The goal should have been impossible to accomplish, or so I first thought. I didn't expect to get results. In fact, I was saying to the universe, this works for everyone but me. I didn't know for sure, but I was acting as if it could be true.

That night, an acquaintance took me to a party. I met Jeff while wandering about. Jeff was recently single, as his girlfriend had just moved out the month before, and he did not enjoy living alone in his elegant apartment in the Marina district overlooking the Bay. I moved in two days later, and instead of paying rent, bought the bare necessities for the refrigerator. Since Jeff never ate at home, I lived there virtually rent-free for six months while I studied for my chiropractic boards. What were the odds of this happening?

Make a list of the things you want but do not yet have. Maybe you want a better job, a new car, a place to call your own, a good relationship, or a better spiritual life. Whatever it is, just put it down on paper.

_____

_____

_____

_____

_____

_____

Close your eyes and take a deep breath. Breathe out fear and limitation, and breathe in new ideas, opportunities, changes, health, wealth, and happiness. Imagine you have the most perfect life. Let's make this image more concrete and real.

Think deeply about what you want. It is not enough to say, "I want a career as a fireman." You must then describe every detail about life as a fireman. Describe exactly what you want, where you will live, how you will look, and what it will feel like.

My ideal job is ...

_____

_____

_____

Visualize. Continue to get even more specific about your life. How many hours do you want to work and when? What part of town do you want to work in? What do you want to wear while on the job? What type of boss are you compatible with? What types of coworkers would you enjoy working with? What type of salary do you want to make? Then take it a step further. What type of neighborhood will you return to at night? What type of lifestyle will you live? Who are your companions? Be very specific in writing down your expectations and desires. Put this list on your mirror and other places that you look at frequently throughout the day.

_____

_____

_____

_____

_____

What can I do right now to start making this dream a reality?

_____

_____

_____

_____

_____

_____

If I could have any car in the world, what would I drive?

_____

Visualize yourself at a car dealership speaking to an employee there. Really *see* yourself on the lot, scanning the vehicles. Then you find that perfect one for you. What color is it? What brand is it? What year was it made? Read the tag. How much does it cost? Forget about your doubts at this point. Envision yourself driving away in the hottest car on the lot.

Describe your perfect car.

_____

_____

_____

So you want a new home? Create a picture in your mind that shows you living this new life. What does the new house look like? How large or small is it? How many stories would you have in your perfect home? What amenities come with it? How have you decorated the inside, and what are you cooking in the kitchen? What does the new place smell like? How does it feel to live in this future home?

Describe these images now.

_____

_____

_____

_____

Your fears and doubts have been supervising you and banning you for years. For just a moment, suspend and ban those fears. For one moment, let your creativity soar without question.

If you could be or do anything in your life, and if you had unlimited funds, and if there were no limitations, how would you spend your time? My perfect life would include:

_____

_____

_____

_____

_____

What would you do, if you had only three years to live?

_____

_____

_____

_____

_____

What would my life be like if I did these things? How would it change?

_____

_____

_____

_____

What has kept me from doing these things?

_____
_____
_____
_____
_____

Now, turn your dreams into real life goals. Make a commitment to work towards those goals. Write down your dream-turned goals.

_____
_____
_____
_____
_____

Which of these things could you begin to do now?

_____
_____
_____

Set your goals high!

Immediate Goals: (Today, tomorrow, this week)

_____
_____
_____
_____
_____

Thirty day goals:

_____
_____
_____
_____ •
_____
_____
_____

One Year Goals:

_____
_____
_____
_____
_____
_____

Five year Goals:

_____
_____
_____
_____
_____
_____

Life Time Goals:

_____
_____
_____
_____
_____

Remember, just because you categorize a goal into a certain time frame, doesn't mean that's when it will necessarily happen. For instance, I've created five-year goals, and just by the simple act of knowing I'd have that, I was able to see it materialize in months. On the flip side, don't get discouraged if your short-term goal doesn't happen immediately. Perhaps there's another goal you need to accomplish first. Just stay focused, and know that someday all of your dreams will come true.

Use this same strategy to attract the relationship you desire. Create two lists. On the first list, create everything you want in a partner. What color eyes do they have? What color is their hair? What body type do they have? What types of clothes do they wear? What do they do for a living? What type of car do they drive? What is their life's purpose? What religion do they practice? How do they smell?

_____

_____

_____

_____

_____

_____

_____

_____

_____

_____

In the second list, describe your ideal relationship. How do you communicate with one another? What activities you do together? Where do you go on vacations? What type of home will you live in together? What things can you create with one another? How do your life's purposes mesh?

_____
_____
_____
_____
_____
_____
_____
_____
_____
_____

What could I do today to attract my partner? What places could I go that I might find this person?

_____
_____
_____
_____
_____
_____

Look for your soul mate,
every evening at sunset,
take time to watch
the changing colors in the heavens.
Send your mating call across the skies
Feel your soul mate's presence, and
Listen inwardly for their call!

Below, I have decided to share some of my goals with you as an example.

JOAN'S LIST:

I want to be a ..

- Great mother
- Founder of the worldwide Miracle Makers Club
- An inspiration to others
- Healer
- Renowned motivational speaker
- Worldwide traveler
- Woman who makes a difference in people's lives
- The host of the hottest television talk show in town that inspires, empowers, excites, revives, renews, recreates, and changes lives.
- Best selling author of many widely read books

I want to have ...

- Ski vacations, adventures, tropical vacations
- Regular, well paid speaking events throughout the country
- A large home with several acres and a pool
- An art studio overlooking a garden
- Dogs, cats, and horses for my growing family
- A personal chef
- Opulent villa in Italy
- My own designer jet plane that whisks my family or entourage anyplace at any time including my dog Bear, so that when we travel, everyone I love and everything I need is at my disposal with minimal inconvenience.

- A chauffeur to drive me everywhere I need to go, allowing me to sit in the back seat and work, talk, or relax.

THE POWER OF YOUR SHOWER

Your shower is a miracle resource. Use your shower to rid yourself of negative emotion by following this daily ritual. Replace your self-critical thinking with positive thoughts. As you stand under your showerhead, imagine that you are washing away your everyday self. Let your worries and concerns dissolve under the stream of flowing water. Visualize the water pouring over you as light energy, cleansing, healing, and bringing forth the goodness you deserve on this planet. Start to believe that health, wealth, and happiness flows through you.

There is a captain who is steering your course—your Higher Self. Allow your true spirit to take charge now. Let that person with the mission and direction, the one who comprehends the larger picture, take control. You are no longer haphazard about accomplishing the things you set out to do. From this shower on, you have the power to create your larger life.

Recently, I have begun to use my shower power in the bathtub. I haven't changed the name yet, but I find that as I soak in the water, I can do the meditation much easier, and invariably, answers and solutions come to mind so quickly, I don't even have time to wipe my hands dry before I am writing ideas down in my journal. I can feel a real sense of self and can absorb positive information like a sponge.

The idea is to visualize the coming day in detail and put an enthusiastic spin on it. See yourself dressing, driving your children to school, going to work, making phone calls, and pushing your agenda forward. Your life is working smoothly, and your self-esteem grows. What would happen in your new utopian life?

_____

_____

_____

_____

_____

_____

Everyday, you can create miracles in the shower as you wash your blues away—or anywhere else, for that matter. See yourself living the life of your dreams.

Your homework is to permit yourself to dream the impossible, and find ways to achieve it. Use affirmations to create the energy to make miracles. These are some of the ones that worked for me.

- I am a magnet for money
- I am a magnet for miracles
- Only good, supportive, loving people come into my life
- I am a shining star
- Every day, in every way, life gets better, better and better
- I am committed to change
- I am a best selling author
- I am a healer and my work inspires others

For this next exercise, create some affirmations of your own and list them below.

- I am _____
- I am _____
- I am _____
- I am _____
- I am _____

During my time in chiropractic school, I used to imagine that I was driving a red sports car, top down, with my hair flying in the wind. I used this image to create success as inspiration to the challenges of being a student in my late twenties. After passing my boards, I decided to buy a red Fiat. I was able to afford it, because I dared to dream it.

It is vital that you determine what you want. Your thoughts are writing your checkbook. If you ask for a life where you just squeak by, then that's what you will get—a tough life. So dream large. If you need $10,000 a month to live on, don't ask for $5,000, or even $9,000, because you won't have enough, and you will continue to feel as if you were in scarcity.

Very few on this planet love the existence they lead. For many, life remains a brutal struggle for survival; rising beyond the mundane, seems a lifetime away and requires an immense effort to overcome extreme challenges. That's why it is important to use visualization to create your innermost dreams. Give yourself permission to create big pictures. Create it first in the inner realms, and you will then create success on the outer. Your level of prosperity is directly related to your inner visions of health, wealth, and happiness and the amounts you feel you deserve.

T. Harv Eker, author of *Secrets of the Millionaire Mind—Mastering the Inner Game of Wealth,* says that becoming rich is a matter of changing your attitudes and beliefs about yourself. He issues a warning in his book. "If you don't do the inner work on yourself and somehow you make a lot of money, it would most likely be a stroke of luck and there's a good chance you'd lose it. But if you become a successful person inside and out, you'll not only make it, you'll keep it, grow it, and become truly happy."

Try this plan if you have lost your dreams and goals. This chapter will help you to overcome problems with your career, your relationships, or your life in general. The plan will give you a solid foundation in case the rug or security blanket disappears. Use this when life slaps you in the face and forces you to get real, quick. Unleash your hidden stores of courage, dig deep, and build a foundation to assist you in surviving crisis and creating a healthier, happier and harmonious life.

Catching a miracle is
like catching a wave.

Perfect timing and proper placement are
required. Be ready to soar at the precise
moment the wave rushes to greet you.

Do not be shy.

If you plan your miracle and position
yourself properly, you will leap through the
air with the greatest of ease
and ride your miracle wave
to the life of your dreams

CREATE A FAMILY PURPOSE AND FAMILY PLAN

*E*VERY FAMILY HAS A UNIQUE PURPOSE, and each individual member has their own mission as well. My family and I had a purpose, which was to create miracles in our lives and share them with the world. As a family, our goal was to be an example to others and to show them that it can be done.

Elana's mission was to find us our new home. She studied magazines and literally devoured books on house plans. She worked very hard to help get us in a better environment. Anton was our activity, event, and adventure coordinator. He loves to rock climb, hike, mountain bike, snowboard, and he is an athletic enthusiast. His role was to plan low budget outings that would challenge us, bring us closer together and raise morale.

The support of your family in the creation of your new life plan is extremely helpful. When you are living your life's purpose, you are naturally feeling better about yourself. Don't you want that for everyone around you as well? The energy required to create a new life is enormous, and at times, it could feel overwhelming and much too great for one person to carry alone. That doesn't mean it is impossible, it just means that you must surround yourself with people on the path of the miraculous, and if you're family isn't already on that path, it is now your responsibility to get them there. You are the one who must be the visionary in your family. Since you're the one absorbing this knowledge, it's your job to guide them. Their support will catapult your life high up into the miracle wave.

If your family is resistant, remember that most people prefer routine and don't necessarily enjoy change. You might know they will love the outcome, but they don't see that. Let them know that it is important for change to come from within the entire family. As a unit, you will be far more effective. It might take them a little time to come around. Lead by example, even when you think no one's looking.

Remember to be patient with those who don't jump on board immediately. Your children's behaviors are reflections of things you've taught them. If you haven't been living your purpose this whole time, and suddenly you decide it's time to start, they might not see the need for it. Changing patterns does take time, and if you try to force them into it, they could be more resistant. If you tell your children that they now have a new chore to do—to make miracles—they might want to run and hide in their rooms. But if you let them know that you're going to play a new game with them, your chances of success will increase.

Have an emergency family meeting. If they appear hesitant, ask them what they think the family purpose should be. Discuss the possibilities and agree on one central mission. Next, define the individual goals, allowing each person to choose his own path. Each family member needs to be encouraged to meet these goals.

If the first meeting doesn't go smoothly, remember this, negativity is contagious, and if there's recently been ill thoughts in the air, they're just reacting to the vibrations. Don't get down about it. They will recover. Positivism will catch on and eventually spread like wildfire. Be gently persistent. A hidden law of the universe says that when you put in order, chaos blows. This is a *good thing*. This is a sign that better times are on the horizon. Let them protest and acknowledge them. Don't turn it into a fight. If you do, you loose.

What is your family's mission statement?

_____

_____

_____

_____

WHO DOES WHAT?

Write a job description for each family member. If you're not sure, ask the individuals how they think they can contribute to your group success.

Parent

_____

_____

_____

_____

Parent

_____
_____
_____
_____

Child

_____
_____
_____
_____

Child

_____
_____
_____
_____

Hold frequent family meetings to update your goals and dreams and keep current with each other's visions. This is a good time to review weekly schedules, chores, and events. Working together, all members of the family can achieve their mutual goals. Strategize with your family so that everyone knows the big picture and how they fit into the outcome. Each member of the team should know the position they play and how to support the others.

We always started with chanting "om", because it sounded good to us and calmed us down until we were ready. Then each of us would share one or two miracles that have happened. Once complete, we would discuss our personal goals and how we are creating our personal success. We then move onto the family goals and how we are working with them.

I was recently asked what happens to your personal goals when you concentrate on family goals. Personal goals and values occur within the context of your family goals. Let's say the family's mission statement is to inspire and heal. Each family member participates in this, as well as completes their own personal mission statement and quest. All of the purposes should merge.

Transformation is a family affair. Your children need to know that although tough times may lie ahead, their family is strong and united. Turn your family into a team. Go through the steps of this workbook with your spouse and your children. The rewards for your work, I promise, are much greater than you've ever imagined.

FAMILY PROJECT

Turn off the television. Shut down the video games. Take the phone off the hook. Set up a sacred time when you can all get together and focus on creating miracles. Provide a large sheet of poster paper for each member of the family and several extras for the group or family projects. Have stacks of magazines laid out on a table, and ask each member to flip through several to collect the pictures and words that inspire them. Build up an extensive collection of fascinating collage materials, and when you are ready, start to create the new life. This activity is especially recommended for the ones who draw a blank when you ask them to define their miracle. Though they may not have the vocabulary to tell you their mission statement, they can certainly tell you what it is that they love to do, and the two are inseparable.

Glue pictures onto the poster boards to represent your family values and spirituality. Glue photos of homes, furnishings, travel itineraries, cars, and all the things you want to have. You get the picture. In doing this, you will be creating your family life map. In the center, place a family portrait, and radiating outward, begin to list all the things that your family wants to be, already has, and intends to do together.

What type of life will you have together?

_____

_____

_____

_____

_____

_____

_____

_____

WARNING: Spending time together working on projects has been known to strengthen family bonds, correct problems, and lessen frustrations. Common side effects include loss of time with video games and television. Do this project at your own risk.

Next, once these miracles start to manifest, hold weekly family meetings to discuss the wins. A win is anything that someone intends to do. So if you intend to get to the grocery store, even though you have a million things to do, and you go, that's a win. If you get to buy your dream house, that's a win. After each person has stood up and said his or her win, have everyone clap. This is a good meeting to include neighbor kids and school friends. You want them to see what you can do when you put your mind to it.

This process of acknowledging what you have done is essential. Commit to this rule: *there will be no mention of losses.* You can discuss a plan to take a failure and turn it into a win, but unlike an AA meeting, this group discussion is not designed to talk about failure or loss. The idea is to uplift and send out positive vibes into the physical universe.

DEVELOP YOUR OVERALL GAME PLAN.
Set family goals and uncover your family mission.

	PARENT	PARENT	CHILD	CHILD
PHYSICAL				
EMOTIONAL				
FINANCIAL				
LIFESTYLE				
HOME				
TRAVEL				
SPIRITUAL				
FUN				

"A good football team relies more on harmonious coordination of effort than individual skill. A winning team is one whose members recognize that when one member of the team is successful, the entire team wins. Conversely, a sure way to develop a losing formula is to create an environment in which team members compete with one another instead of the opponent. When all members give their best in every situation, whether they are carrying the ball or clearing the way for someone else, the team wins and so does each individual member."

—NAPOLEON HILL

What could I do to help my community?

_____

_____

_____

_____

_____

What could I do to help the world?

_____

_____

_____

_____

_____

Imagine this strong, positive energy is contagious and spreads throughout the entire world. Each person you encounter catches the vibration and radiates outward to others as this uplifting feeling magnifies. You are a powerful source of energy, capable of transforming and uplifting the world. You *can* make a difference.

If you do these things, you will finally know what it means to make miracles. But don't take my word for it. Go out there and apply this information. The only way you'll ever know for certain is to observe yourself doing it.

༺

TRIUMPH OVER TRAGEDY

*I*N NOVEMBER OF 2004, I finally received my settlement from UnumProvident. A judge awarded me 7.7 million dollars in punitive damages and bad faith fraudulent practices. The Ninth Circuit Appellate Court upheld the judgment in a three-judge unanimous ruling and wrote a long written opinion to go with it. This opinion has been cited in courtrooms around the country.

Since then, a mandatory 45-state investigation re-opened over 112,000 cases which had closed after 2000. UnumProvident was fined fifteen million dollars. In addition, California fined them eight million dollars.

In a glorious moment of turn-around, I was invited to the press conference held by California State Insurance Commissioner, John Garamendi, to announce the results of the investigations into UnumProvident's claims practices. It was held on the steps of the federal court building where my lawsuit had been heard. I was gratified to hear him tell Unum shape up or ship out of California. It was a dream come true for me to be next to him and to be allowed to share my story.

We did two press conferences that day—one in San Francisco and another in L.A. I rode in the commissioner's chauffeured car to the airport. Mr. Garamendi told me that my story and my case was inspirational to him and those he worked with.

In Los Angeles, I stood at the podium with an array of cameras and videos recording the event. At long last, I was able to share my tragic story with the world. Finally, people listened to what I had to say, and it felt so good. During my talk, I spoke about all the claimants who have had their benefits wrongfully denied and the lives that have been destroyed by the callous treatment of their insurance company. I spoke in honor of the people who did not yet have a voice. And then I spoke about the Miracle Makers Club.

I cried during the press conference. I had imagined this day in my mind so often, as a dream, a fantasy ... I'd always wondered what it would feel like, and here I was living it. And just as I'm thinking, does life get any better than this? It did.

I received a phone call from Michael, an assistant producer at CBS. He said that they were interested in covering my experiences with Unum on national television. I felt as if something important would happen from this type of story. Ed Bradley from *Sixty Minutes* interviewed me for their exposé. You have no idea how gratifying this felt. As it turned out, my interview got cut, but the program still aired, and in the end, the bad guys were held accountable for the wrongful injuries they created.

The best part of all of my troubles and triumphs is that I have begun to love and value myself. I have actually become an incredibly interesting, fascinating, intense, unique person. One of the most astonishing results of these past few years is that I now have an active voice. I am no longer passive or afraid to tell the world what I think.

I am now living the life I envisioned in my dreams.

Every week brings new and exciting ideas. Last month I spoke with the producer of *Teen Talk* in LA. She loved my story about how the kids and I formed the Miracle Makers Club, and she wants Elana, Anton, and I on her television show. Now that is exciting! We get to share how we used the Miracle Makers Club to reshape our life with others. We envisioned we would do this seven years ago, and now here we are doing it.

I started a website dedicated to the Unum victims, and I've had the great fortune of being able to communicate and help many of them. I hope to someday launch a full program for them so that they can rebuild their lives as I've done.

My life has become an absolute miracle. From the moment I committed to making my dreams a reality, there was no turning back. I went on faith alone, and now I can tell you it was worth every penny, every pain, every second of sacrifice and suffering. I have come so far. And as time goes on, I continue to live my dream of healing and inspiring others.

As the scene goes in *Alice and Wonderland,* the Queen is baffled by Alice's failure to be able to make things happen. The Queen tells her that she is able to do eight impossible things before breakfast each day. You too have this ability. Eliminate the word impossible from your vocabulary and replace it with possibilities.

This life is what you make it. I challenge you to dream the impossible, do the unthinkable, and live the fantasy life you've always wanted. I give to you, the gift of knowing how to make miracles.

SEVEN DAY JOURNAL

What is a Miracle Journal? Well, it is a couple of things: First, it is a place to write down and keep safe your hopes, wishes, and dreams, and second it is a place to really take stock of your life. Writing anchors in what you want. It's a direct communication with the universe around you and assists you in attracting the things that matter most. You can have a Miraculous Day, everyday!

Day One: Date _____

List every mini-miracle or lucky miracle that comes your way today. If there were not that many note-worthy events that happened today, think back to the most memorable throughout your life and record what happened below. Before each one, state which type of miracle it is.

This activity is for you to do over and over—each day, if time permits. You might be interested to learn that as time goes on, your answer to this question will change drastically, as your awareness arises. Keep copious notes, and after quite a bit of time has gone by, look back to your first entries and compare them to the latest and greatest.

_____

_____

_____

_____

_____

_____

_____

_____

_____

_____

_____

_____

_____

_____

_____

_____

_____

_____

_____

_____

Day Two: Date _____

Ask yourself what if you had made a different decision. The object of this process is to recognize the things that you would like to change; that you feel like you could have or should have done differently. You will want to create your own questions based on key turning points in your life. I have made a list of examples to give you ideas.

What if …

- I had married the person down the street?
- I didn't marry at all? Where would I be now?
- I had chosen to go to college?
- I had taken that new job?
- I had won the lottery?
- we had another baby?
- I had waited to have children or start a family?
- I knew then what I know now?

_____

_____

_____

_____

_____

_____

_____

_____

_____

_____

_____

_____

_____

Day Three: Date _____

Assess your current situation. Make a list of the things that you do not like about your life. Your list could include twenty items or two. Just be honest about every aspect that needs a miracle touch.

_____

_____

_____

_____

_____

_____

_____

_____

_____

_____

_____

_____

_____

_____

_____

_____

_____

_____

_____

_____

_____

_____

_____

_____

_____

_____

_____

_____

What have you learned from the problems that you have created? What parts of your life, as it is now, could you use to make a difference to others?

_____
_____
_____
_____
_____
_____
_____
_____
_____
_____
_____
_____
_____
_____
_____
_____
_____
_____
_____
_____
_____
_____
_____
_____
_____
_____

Recognize the positive things you have already created in your life. What miracles have you created that you would like to create again? When you are finished, just decide that you will do it again. Don't consider the problems that could come up. If you did it once, you can do it again.

_____
_____
_____
_____
_____
_____
_____
_____
_____
_____
_____
_____
_____
_____
_____
_____
_____
_____
_____
_____
_____
_____
_____
_____
_____
_____

Day Six: Date _____

By now, you've hopefully established your mission in life. If you have not, ask yourself, what are my top three things to do? Your life's purpose likely lives within the answer. Below, make a list of positive affirmations that will help you to accomplish your goals.

_____
_____
_____
_____
_____
_____
_____
_____
_____
_____
_____
_____
_____
_____
_____
_____
_____
_____
_____
_____
_____
_____
_____
_____
_____
_____

Day Seven: Date _____

What could I do to help my family? How could I help the people in my community? How could I make a difference, using my purpose, to affect my country? In what ways could I change the world?

_____
_____
_____
_____
_____
_____
_____
_____
_____
_____
_____
_____
_____
_____
_____
_____
_____
_____
_____
_____
_____
_____
_____
_____
_____
_____
_____

Extra Notes on Miracles:

Extra Notes on Miracles:

MIRACLE DICTIONARY

Miracle Allies—those people who are in your life to assist you in your quest. These people might pave the way, assist you, or give you moral support. One of my friends met the producer of a national TV show at a party, and within ten days she accepted the role of cat woman because of it. Another friend met a board member for a local school district at a luncheon. This chance meeting gave her inroads to the exact school she wanted to attend. Miracle allies come when we have raised our vibration to attract the positive reflections back to us. You have the ability to be a miracle ally to someone else.

Miracle Buddies—friends that help keep you on your right path. They know that you have unlimited possibilities to live your life to the fullest, and they are willing to support you in reaching your highest dreams. Visualize and set goals with this person to enhance your energy and raise your frequency to attract what you want.

Miracle Brew—essential ingredients for your transformation. The brew includes a little bit of courage, part faith, deep breathes, visualization and imagery, affirmations, and goal setting, and anything else that creates a new mind set and vibration for you. These ingredients get stirred into the miracle pot. The result is miraculous.

Miracle Busters—people who trip you up and want to see you fail. They can be family or friends who profess to love you but don't understand that you need to reach for the highest level to achieve your potential this life. They mistakenly encourage you to take bad advice, go into the wrong profession, and worry about your future. They will tell you that you can't have your dream. Do not share goals, hopes, dreams or desires with miracle busters. When you are with miracle busters, you will notice you feel depressed, moody, fearful, and invalidated.

Miracle Mandate—The miracle mandate says that each of us has the potential to live the life we dream. If we follow our quest, we will transform our life to a more prosperous level, This mandate is within each one of you. Think of it this way, it is your destiny to live a prosperous, loving, successful, abundant life. You have the seeds of unlimited potential within you.

Miracle Pot—the miracle pot holds the brew and the ingredients. All we need to do is grab hold of it and stir.

Miracle Wave—the miracle wave is that forward wave of momentum that sweeps you off of your feet with its force. Suddenly everything goes your way, and you are attracting far greater things than you even imagined. You find yourself meeting the right person, getting the job you covet, or meeting your soul mate by chance at Starbucks. The universe literally lines up to give you more of what you are wanting. Road blocks seemingly disappear. Its as if the world around you is saying yes to *all* of your requests and postulates.

Miracle Wand—similar to a lightening rod. It conducts a positive wave of energy attracting to you that which you desire.the miracle wand serves two purposes. Use it as a reminder that you can create miracles. Last month I was in the rainforest with my two teenagers, about to be attached to a cable so that I could swing over the waterfall, 300 feet below. I grabbed the miracle wand in my back pocket, reaffirming the words: I can do this. I love to fly. I am an unlimited being capable of all things. The wand became my reminder of my inner resources. Use it when feeling scared, confused, depressed, or doubtful. The miracle wand can also be used as a conduit of energy. For example, when affirming I am a magnet for miracles, trace a dollar sign five times with your wand. This creates an intention in the universe that sees and knows wealth and prosperity.

Miraculous—Living your life at a level that is beyond your wildest dreams. All systems in the universe are telling you to keep on going, because you are manifesting those dreams you had hidden inside. That is a miraculous life, when you wake up in the morning excited and passionate about your life.

Mundane—a life style that is not fulfilling your higher calling. It leaves you feeling numb, bored, unsatisfied, moody, depressed, impoverished, ill, or whatever else you can come up with that keeps you from following your dream. At this point you could be anything from impoverished and desperate, to financially successfully but spiritually uneasy. Learning to live and navigate the realities of life are important, but equally important is to follow your intuition and guidance, and ask the question, does it make my heart sing. If the answer is no, something must change immediately.

Vibration—Everything in the universe vibrates at a certain frequency. Even solid objects are made up of electrons, protons, and neutrons in constant motion. Each person has a specific energy frequency that is radiated outward into the universe. One clue to your vibrational level is your emotional states. Depression, apathy, and rage are a lower state vibrations. Confidence, love, joy, and happiness are indications that you are raising your vibration and energy.

Carry the book with you
and take copious notes.
Write down your impressions.
Design your future!

ABOUT THE AUTHOR

Dr Joan Hangarter, D.C, M.S., is an author, inspirational speaker, coach, doctor of chiropractic, and host of the successful radio show, "Make Your Miracle Today." In 1998 she founded The Miracle Makers Club as a way to overcome tremendous obstacles and now shares these amazing techniques with all of us.

HOW TO CONTACT THE AUTHOR

For more information,
to have Joan speak to your organization,
conduct workshops, or order more books contact:

The Miracle Makers Club
P.O. Box 2527
Novato, CA 94948
415-883-0810
drjoanr@miraclemakersclub.com

Visit our website at
www.miraclemakersclub.com

SPEAKER TOPICS

The Miracle Makers Club

You were borne to create a fulfilling and prosperous life and achieve your unique destiny.

- How to begin to speak the miracle language.
- Understand your path to your miraculous life.
- How to have a miraculous day every day.
- Raise your vibration to catch your miracle wave.

Benefits

- Learn the four types of miracles and how to recognize and attract your share.
- Step by step process to raise your vibration and catch your miracle wave.
- Create health, wealth and happiness now.
- Learn how to flex your miracle muscle and activate your inner potential.
- Go from mundane to miraculous instantaneously.
- Become a magnet for miracles.
- Become a part of a global transformational force to achieve world wide miracles.

To Book Dr. Joan for your group,
contact her at
drjoan@miraclemakersclub.com
or call today at **415-883-0810**

WHY JOIN THE MIRACLE MAKERS CLUB?

*As you step into your own power you become
a member of the Miracle Makers Club*

I believe you already have everything you need inside you to create a prosperous, loving, mindful life. However, you haven't yet been given the tools to unlock the miracle-making secrets. That's what we do in the **Miracle Makers Club**. We share the secrets, the strategies and the techniques to help you stir the miracle brew.

Miracle-Makers share their miracles and express their dreams or visions in such a manner that it positively impacts others. The contribution could come in many ways: through healing, mentoring, expressing or teaching in some manner that spreads transformation and joy.

Imagine the waves of the sea, emanating from their center and reaching distant shores. That is the effect of a miracle being spread throughout the world.

When you join the **Miracle Makers Club** you receive the tools that bring you closer to living your own miraculous life. What I share in the SEVEN-DAY MIRACLE PLAN alone will literally raise your vibration to attract your dreams. And I have also included specific techniques such as the MIRACLE ACTIVATION MEDITATION, designed to literally awaken your sleeping miracle-making self. The journals help you record your findings and create action plans to put your dreams into motion.

ENROLL NOW IN THE MIRACLE MAKERS CLUB AND YOU'LL ALSO RECEIVE $313.75 IN FREE BONUS TOOLS CREATED TO ACCELERATE YOUR TRANSFORMATION

Bonus Tool 1—A SEVEN DAY MIRACLE PLAN Created by Dr Joan ($12.95 value). This seven-day letter series is designed to transform your life one day at a time.

Bonus Tool 2—A SEVEN DAY COMPANION JOURNAL ($12.95 value). The companion piece to the Journal gives you a place to record your miracles and produce action plans.

Bonus Tool 3—The MIRACLE ACTIVATION JOURNAL and CD with music by Gail Muldrow ($38.00 value) With this guided meditation CD and companion journal, you will embark upon a 4-step, life-altering journey. This kit provides the building blocks for miracle-makers in training.

Bonus Tool 4—*AGAINST ALL ODDS* by Cathleen Fillmore ($14.95). This riveting book is packed with true stories that will make you laugh and cry, and ultimately, take your breath away. Written by Cathleen Fillmore, *Against All Odds* depicts the stories of ordinary people doing extraordinary things. People who had no idea of the depth of their inner resources until life severely tested them. Dr Joan's personal journey is included in this inspiring anthology.

Bonus Tool 5—SIX MONTH MIRACLE TIDBITS PROGRAM ($19.95 value). Every morning in your email box you will find a miracle tidbit, an encouraging and inspirational message from Dr Joan to help you continue to raise your vibration.

Bonus Tool 6—THE MIRACLE NEWSLETTER ($49.95 value). Weekly insights and exact steps for achieving your transformation from Dr Joan.

Bonus Tool 7—$25.00 COUPON for your first Miracle Activation Reading. Because we want you to become Miracle-Makers, if you need additional one-on-one time, you will receive a $25.00 discount on our regular miracle activation fees. We love you so much we want to help you succeed in initiating your personal miracles. The readings are designed to break through any obstacles to your success!

Bonus 8—50% DISCOUNT for 360 Days of Membership to The Miracle Makers Club ($140.00 value) Our new club is jam-packed with resources . Learn how to recognize a miracle, and get the tools you need to master the four types of miracles. Take your miracle meter and use your own natural cycles and rhythms to achieve your dreams. Link and mastermind with others striving to build new lives. Share your miracle stories. These are just a few of the benefits.

Sign up today! All this is valued at $313.75 prior to shipping costs so take advantage of this wonderful offer and start changing your life today. To get all this and more, your special cost is only $79.95 shipping included.

Simply go to our website at www.miraclemakersclub.com and follow the links to Join the **Miracle Makers Club** or for more information email us at info@miraclemakersclub.com miraclemakersclub.com

PSIA information can be obtained
www.ICGtesting.com
inted in the USA
SOW01n1759190516
631FS

C
an
Pl
Fs
20